Enhancing Adolescents' Motivation for Science

Classroom Insights from Educational Psychology Series

A Developmental Approach to
Educating Young Children
Denise H. Daniels and Patricia K. Clarkson

Transforming Teaching and Learning
Through Data-Driven Decision Making
Ellen B. Mandinach and Sharnell S. Jackson

An Interpersonal Approach to
Classroom Management: Strategies
for Improving Student Engagement
*Heather A. Davis, Jessica J. Summers,
and Lauren M. Miller*

Engaging Young Children
With Informational Books
Helen Patrick and Panayota Mantzicopoulos

Enhancing Adolescents'
Motivation for Science
Lee Shumow and Jennifer A. Schmidt

Enhancing Adolescents'
Motivation
for **Science**

Research-Based Strategies for Teaching
Male and Female Students

Lee Shumow
Jennifer A. Schmidt

Foreword by Shawn M. Glynn

A Joint Publication

CORWIN
A SAGE Company

FOR INFORMATION:

Corwin

A SAGE Company

2455 Teller Road

Thousand Oaks, California 91320

(800) 233-9936

www.corwin.com

SAGE Publications Ltd.

1 Oliver's Yard

55 City Road

London EC1Y 1SP

United Kingdom

SAGE Publications India Pvt. Ltd.

B 1/I 1 Mohan Cooperative Industrial Area

Mathura Road, New Delhi 110 044

India

SAGE Publications Asia-Pacific Pte. Ltd.

3 Church Street

#10-04 Samsung Hub

Singapore 049483

Acquisitions Editor: Jessica Allan

Associate Editor: Kimberly Greenberg

Project Editor: Amy Schroller

Copy Editor: Erin Livingston

Typesetter: C&M Digitals (P) Ltd.

Proofreader: Jennifer Grubba

Indexer: Maria Sosnowski

Cover Designer: Candice Harman

This material is based upon work supported by the National Science Foundation under Grant No: HRD-0827526. Any opinions, findings, conclusions, or recommendations expressed in this material are those of the authors and do not reflect the views of the National Science Foundation.

Printed in the United States of America.

A catalog record of this book is available from the Library of Congress.

ISBN 978-1-4522-6969-6

This book is printed on acid-free paper.

SUSTAINABLE FORESTRY INITIATIVE
Certified Chain of Custody
Promoting Sustainable Forestry
www.sfiprogram.org
SFI-01268

SFI label applies to text stock

15 16 17 10 9 8 7 6 5 4 3 2

Contents

Lists of Figures and Tables   ix

Foreword   xi
Shawn M. Glynn

Series Preface to *Classroom Insights*   xiii
Debra K. Meyer and Lynley H. Anderman

Preface   xvii

    Enhancing Motivational
      Knowledge and Practices   xix
    Overview of Chapters   xxi

Acknowledgments   xxiii

About the Authors   xxvii

1. Introduction: Motivation to Learn Science   1
    The SciMo Project   2
    How Time Was Used in Classrooms   3
    The Student Perspective on High School
      Science Classes   5
    Gender Differences in Student Motivation
      and Perspective   6
    The Experience of Boys and Girls in Science   8
    Gender and Teacher-Student Interaction   10
    The Importance of Promoting Gender
      Equity in Science   11
    What Resources Can Science Teachers Use
      to Get More Background Information?   11

2. Value   **13**
What Does It Mean to Value Science?   13
Why Is Valuing Science Important?   16
What Have Researchers Discovered about
     Valuing Science in Classrooms?   17
How Can Teachers Foster Value?   20
What Resources Can Science Teachers
     Use to Promote Value?   25

3. Affiliation   **27**
What Do Classroom Social Relationships
     Include in High School?   28
Why Are Classroom Social Relationships Important?   30
What Have Researchers Discovered about Classroom
     Relationships in Science?   31
How Can Teachers Build Positive Relationships with
     and Among Their Students?   36
What Resources Can Science Teachers
     Use to Understand and Build Positive Relationships?   39

4. Autonomy   **41**
What Is Autonomy?   41
Why Is Autonomy Important?   42
What Have Researchers Discovered about
     Autonomy in Science Classrooms?   44
How Can Teachers Foster Autonomy?   49
What Resources Are Available to Science Teachers for
     Promoting Student Autonomy?   54

5. Confidence   **55**
What Does It Mean to Have Confidence
     in Scientific Abilities?   56
Why Is Confidence Important?   56
What Have Researchers Discovered about Confidence?   57
How Can Teachers Build Student Confidence?   62
What Resources Can Science Teachers Use to Promote
     Confidence?   65

6. Success   **67**
What Is the Motivational Concept of Success?   67
Why Is Success an Important Motivational Concept?   69
What Have Researchers Discovered about
     Success in Science Classrooms?   70

How Can Teachers Promote Student Success
    and Encourage Motivating Attributions?   72
What Resources Can Science Teachers
    Use to Promote Success?   77

7. Goal Orientation   **79**
What Is Goal Orientation?   79
Why Is Goal Orientation Important?   80
What Have Researchers Discovered
    about Goals in Science Classrooms?   83
How Can Teachers Influence
    Students' Goal Orientation?   86
What Resources Can Science Teachers
    Use to Foster Adaptive Goal Orientations?   93

8. Ability Beliefs   **95**
What Are Ability Beliefs?   95
Why Are Ability Beliefs Important?   97
What Have Researchers Discovered
    about Ability Beliefs in Science Classrooms?   100
How Can Teachers Foster Ability Beliefs
    Conducive to Success in Science?   104
What Resources Can Science Teachers
    Use to Understand and Promote Growth
    Mindset and Reduce Stereotype Threat?   109

9. Challenge   **111**
What Is Challenge?   111
Why Is Challenge Important?   112
What Have Researchers Discovered about
    Challenge in Science Classrooms?   114
How Can Teachers Provide Appropriate
    Challenges for Their Students?   119
What Resources Can Science Teachers Use to
    Promote Positive Challenge?   123

10. Emotion   **125**
What Emotions Are Likely to Impact
    Motivation in Science?   125
Why Are Student Emotions Important for High School
    Science Teachers to Consider?   127
What Have Researchers Discovered
    about Student Emotion in Science Class?   129

How Can Teachers Enhance Enjoyment
   and Teach Coping Skills?   134
What Resources Can Science Teachers
   Use to Promote Enjoyment and Decrease Anxiety?   137

Appendix   **139**
Methodology of the SciMo Study   139

References   **147**

Index   **165**

Lists of Figures and Tables

Figure 1.1 How Science Teachers Spend
Their Classroom Time   3

Figure 1.2 Purpose of Teacher Talk   4

Figure 1.3 Thought Experiment: Gender and Science
Achievement   7

Figure 1.4 How Boys and Girls Feel in Science Class   9

Figure 2.1 Techniques for Promoting Relevance   22

Figure 3.1 Student-Teacher Interaction Dimensions
That Foster Student Achievement   34

Figure 4.1 Suggestions for Autonomy-Supportive
Teaching   49

Figure 6.1 Suggestions for Promoting Student Success   73

Figure 6.2 How Different Teacher Attribution
Statements Impact Student Motivation   74

Figure 7.1 Examples of Mastery-Oriented and
Performance-Oriented Feedback   90

Figure 8.1 Fixed and Growth Mindsets Compared   98

Figure 8.2 Techniques That Reduce Stereotype Threat   107

Figure 9.1 The Impact of Challenge and Skill on Students'
Engagement, Success, and Learning   116

Figure 9.2   Perceived Challenge in Various
Science Activities   117

Figure 9.3   High School Students' Engagement at
Different Levels of Challenge   119

Figure 10.1   How Students Feel in Various
Science Activities   130

Figure 10.2   Gender Differences in How Students
Feel During Science Instruction   132

Figure A.1   Students' Educational Expectations   142

Table 7.1   Indicators of Students' Goal
Orientation in Science   85

Table A.1   Participants in the SciMo Study   140

Foreword

This is an impressive book. If you are a high school science teacher, Lee Shumow and Jennifer Schmidt have written this book for you. One of the greatest challenges you face as a teacher is how to motivate *all* of your students—girls and boys—to learn science. In this book, Shumow and Schmidt help you to meet this challenge by sharing with you advances in motivation theory, research, and exemplary practices. They give particular attention to the role of gender. Their research on how best to motivate high school students to learn science has been supported by grants from the National Science Foundation.

Science motivation is important because it fuels *scientific literacy*, which is the understanding of scientific concepts and processes required for making personal decisions, participating in societal affairs, and contributing to economic productivity. Scientific literacy benefits your students who aspire to be future scientists. But, just as importantly, scientific literacy benefits *all* of your students, because science plays an important role in careers of all kinds.

You will find this to be a highly readable book. It is clearly written, free from jargon, conversational in style, and very engaging. In general, the authors take an evidence-based approach to the recommendations they make about how you can motivate your students to learn science. This book is organized into ten chapters, and each one is a gem. Each chapter focuses on a key concept that has been recognized in contemporary national science standards as important in increasing students' motivation. Each chapter begins with an engaging vignette—based on the actual experiences of high school teachers—that illustrates the key concept, provides a rationale for its importance, describes the research that supports it, and offers advice on how best to apply it. The chapters describe and illustrate proven motivational strategies that are designed to foster high achievement in both girls and boys. The strategies are based on a sophisticated understanding of variations in the attitudes, beliefs, and backgrounds of girls and boys learning science.

Throughout this book, Shumow and Schmidt write with a deep understanding of the challenges that you face as a high school science teacher. These challenges are many, such as large class size, limited instructional resources, and students who vary considerably in their preparation and backgrounds. This state-of-the-art book will help both new and seasoned teachers to meet these challenges. This book, written by two nationally recognized experts in educational research, will help science teachers foster students' motivation and scientific literacy.

Shawn M. Glynn

Josiah Meigs Distinguished Teaching Professor

Department of Educational Psychology

Department of Mathematics and Science Education

University of Georgia

Series Preface to *Classroom Insights*

D ivision 15, Educational Psychology, of the American Psychological Association and Corwin partnered to create the *Classroom Insights from Educational Psychology* series for teachers in an effort to reduce the widening gap between research and theory on learning, teaching, and classroom practice. Educational psychology is a discipline that seeks to understand the integration among human development and learning, classroom learning environments and instructional strategies, and student learning and assessment. In this way, the field of educational psychology is among the most relevant and applicable for teachers.

While we have seen great advances in our understanding of student learning and instructional practices over the last decade, these advances are not highly visible in today's classrooms, preservice and graduate teacher education programs, or professional development for teachers. Consequently, classroom practice, for the most part, does not seem to be highly influenced by current research and theory in educational psychology. Yet there are international calls for scientifically based practices, research-based methods, or evidence-based decisions in our schools. As part of the solution to this problem, this series of short, easily accessible books for teachers is designed to synthesize in-depth, high-quality research, to be used in a variety of educational settings, and is endorsed by Division 15.

As the *Classroom Insights* series evolves from its first volumes under founding editor, Dr. Barbara McCombs, we as editors continue to work with teachers and researchers to identify the topics that are most relevant to educators. We are guided by research that honors the highest-quality learning environments with practices proven to support all students, help them succeed in their schooling, and sustain their love of learning. The goals of this series are threefold:

- To give practicing and preservice teachers access to current advances in research and theory on classroom teaching and learning in an easily understood and usable form
- To align educator preparation, graduate study, and professional development with current advances in research and theory, which have not been widely shared with teachers
- To highlight how the most effective teaching practices are based upon a substantial research base and created within classrooms, rather than applied in a "one-size-fits-all" or "silver bullet" approach across classrooms

Classroom Insights provides a series of specialized books to inform teaching and learning in Pre-K–12 classrooms by focusing on what is most important and relevant to today's teachers. In some volumes, the applications are limited to specific age levels or characteristics of students, while in most volumes, the ideas can be broadly applied across Pre-K–12 settings. Classroom strategies are integrated throughout every book, and each includes a wide array of resources for teachers to use to study their practices and improve student achievement and classroom learning environments. Finally, many of these research-based applications will be new approaches and frameworks that have never been published in a series for teachers.

As series editors, our goal is to provide the most up-to-date professional series of teacher resources for connecting teachers with the highest quality and most relevant research in our field of educational psychology. We have planned for every page to provide useful insights for teachers into their current practices in ways that will help them transform classroom learning for their students, themselves, and their school communities.

Sincerely, Your Series Editors

Debra K. Meyer, PhD

Professor

Elmhurst College

Lynley H. Anderman, PhD

Professor

The Ohio State University

Preface

"My students just aren't motivated to learn science."

How many times have you thought or said this? If you are like most science teachers we have spoken with, your answer is "often." Motivating high school students to learn is a primary concern of educators today and a challenge that many science teachers face daily in their classrooms. While it is certainly frustrating to have students who are apathetic toward learning, the good news is that teachers can have a significant impact on the way students approach learning tasks. Put simply, student motivation is something that you can influence. The purpose of this book is to help you learn more about how you can accomplish this. The primary title we have chosen for this book reflects the ultimate goal: *Enhancing Adolescents' Motivation for Science.* In the two years that we have spent researching and writing this book and developing its companion materials, we have come to refer to this whole endeavor using the acronym for "empowering teachers to enhance adolescents' motivation for science", the E-TEAMS Project.

In order to teach effectively, science teachers must integrate knowledge about science content, instructional methods, and student learning, motivation, and development (Davis, Petish, & Smithey, 2006). In a recent study, high school science teachers agreed with the teachers we interviewed, saying they knew little about how to motivate their students. This is especially troubling, because the research shows that when teachers know more about motivation, their students are actually more motivated and more academically successful in science (Hardre & Sullivan, 2009).

Gender is often an important factor in motivation for learning science. As a science teacher, you are likely aware that there have historically been gender gaps with respect to students' attitudes, achievement, and persistence in science. Because of these differences, many of which still exist today, the tools that are most effective at enhancing boys' motivation for science are sometimes (though not always) different than those that work best to boost girls' motivation. It is only logical after all, that if boys and girls have different experiences, attitudes, or expectations about science, the kinds of factors that would motivate them to engage in science should differ somewhat as well. We highlight gender differences throughout the book when research suggests that special attention to student gender is warranted.

Although there are many resources for teachers on fostering student motivation in general, our search did not reveal any books written specifically for science teachers or science teacher educators. It seemed important, then, to provide such a book together with companion materials targeted specifically for the high school science educator to address the unique motivational challenges their students present. Science teachers at other grade levels can glean helpful information from this book as well.

This book has been written for aspiring science teachers, practicing science teachers, and science teacher educators to help you learn more about motivating both male and female high school students to learn science. Each chapter and its supporting materials aim to enhance your understanding of motivational constructs that operate in science classrooms by

- describing and demonstrating useful motivational strategies in science classrooms,
- promoting your understanding of the student perspective on high school science classes,
- sensitizing you to possible gender differences in student motivation and perspective, and
- describing how you can make classroom experiences in science more equitable.

Ultimately, your knowledge about student motivation and how to enhance it in practice can positively influence your students' motivation for science. In the process, you can help increase your students' interest and persistence in fields related to science, technology, engineering, and mathematics (STEM) and narrow gender gaps in students' motivation to pursue science at a higher level.

All of these end-states are consistent with the goals outlined in the Next Generation Science Standards (NGSS), which were being finalized and implemented when this book was published. While we believe the material in this book transcends any set of content standards, the tools provided in this book can be used to support the NGSS by facilitating the progression of knowledge in order to prepare students for deeper levels of science investigation over time. The focus on gender also supports NGSS, as females are a traditionally underrepresented group in most science fields.

This book can be used independently, as part of a professional learning community (PLC), or as a text in a formal science education class. We expect that most teachers reading this book will be interested in achieving most or all of the aforementioned goals, and the book can certainly be read in its entirety in this pursuit. However, busy teachers might not have the time to read, retain, and apply all of the content at once. Therefore, we tried to design each chapter to stand alone in such a way that readers could pick it up, look up a specific aspect of motivation, learn about it, and use its resources without having read prior chapters. The book and its accompanying resources, described below, were designed to allow you to consult and use the materials selectively to meet your needs as they arise in the classroom or as a supplement to other science education texts.

ENHANCING MOTIVATIONAL KNOWLEDGE AND PRACTICES

We wrote this book to provide insight into student perspectives on high school science classes, to provide background information on motivation among male and female students in those classes, and to suggest concrete ideas about how to positively impact student motivation for science.

Structure of the Book

Each chapter concentrates on a single construct that has been widely shown to influence student motivation to learn and that has been shown to be heavily influenced by teacher practices. We realize that there are many aspects of students' lives that can get in the way of their learning, and many of these things cannot be changed by teachers. However, each chapter focuses on those things that teachers can influence, regardless of their students' personal circumstances. Chapter topics were chosen based on our observations in high school science classrooms and in consultation with high school science teachers, science teacher educators, gender scholars, and experts in motivation to learn science.

Within each chapter, we define the motivational construct under consideration and provide an illustrative explanation of how it is important to high school science teachers and students. These examples are drawn from observations we have made in our research: Some are loosely based on our observations, while others are verbatim accounts taken from video data. We briefly summarize the research related to each construct and discuss implications for motivating boys and girls in high school science. We have tried to present motivational processes in science in a way that is accessible, practical, transcendent of specific learning standards, and useful for a variety of stakeholders. Further, we aim to empower you to motivate your students with your teaching practices. We provide suggestions for evidence-based practice, drawing upon our own research and that of other experts in the field.

Companion Materials

A variety of multimedia resources supporting the book are available through our website, http://www.niu.edu/eteams. The site contains brief video clips of real students, teachers, and scientists demonstrating and reflecting upon the constructs described in the book or using our suggestions for practice. These video clips are linked to the book chapters, with each chapter having one or more associated video clips. The website also presents video profiles of the featured science teachers and scientists so that viewers interested in focusing their attention on a broad array of motivational topics within particular areas of specialization (e.g., AP biology or particle physics) can easily do this. Additional resource links and future reading suggestions are provided to accompany each book chapter. PowerPoint presentations are provided for intended use in science department meetings, PLCs, or science education classrooms. These presentations summarize the material in the book, have hyperlinks to the video demonstrations and other relevant material, and include optional discussion or reflection activities for audience members. Parent education resources also are available. We provide several short newsletter articles for families of high school students, focused on enhancing their child's motivation and interest in science. Science teachers or school administrators can post these on school websites or distribute them to students' families. URLs for websites that have specific science-related activities for families appear on the companion website. All of the material on the E-TEAMS website will continue to be updated as we become aware of new resources.

OVERVIEW OF CHAPTERS

In the first chapter, we introduce the concept of motivation as it pertains to science in particular. We also describe the Science-in-the-Moment (SciMo) Project—a research study we conducted in high school classrooms. We draw upon data from the SciMo Project to illustrate many of the motivational processes we discuss throughout the book. This chapter provides a brief introduction to the methodology and primary results from the study, with more detailed methodological information provided in the appendix. Chapters 2 through 10 are focused on specific motivational constructs and processes. As you read them, you will note that they often cross-reference each other, as many of them are related. Chapter 2 focuses on the various ways students might find value in science and how teachers can promote the value and relevance of science in a way that engages and excites students. Chapter 3 deals with relationships in the classroom and discusses how teachers can create a positive classroom climate and foster positive relationships with and among their students. Chapter 4 introduces the concept of autonomy and offers suggestions about how science teachers can afford their students a sense of choice and control while still meeting learning objectives. Chapter 5 discusses multiple strategies for building students' confidence in science and illustrates the positive effects this can have on student performance and engagement. In Chapter 6, we consider student success: While we all want our students to be successful, certain types of successes are more motivating than others, and the way we interpret and explain our success (and our failures) is critical for continued motivation. This chapter discusses what teachers can do to get the most out of their students' successes. Chapter 7 focuses on the types of goals that students have when they are doing their academic work. We discuss goals that are focused primarily on understanding compared to goals that are simply about performing well. We discuss the motivational implications of these different goal orientations and offer suggestions as to how teachers can structure their classrooms in ways that promote productive goals among their students. In Chapter 8, we discuss the different ways students think about the nature of ability. Some students view their science ability as fixed and unchangeable, while others believe their science ability can grow. These different mindsets have dramatic effects on students' motivation and achievement. Chapter 9 provides a discussion of the impact of challenge on student engagement and provides some tips for constructing science learning environments that are optimally challenging for students. Finally, in Chapter 10, we discuss the role of emotions in learning and motivation in science. We discuss the impact of both positive emotions such as enjoyment and negative emotions such as anxiety. At the end of the book, we provide an appendix, which includes a more detailed description of the methodology of the SciMo Project for those who are interested in additional information.

Acknowledgments

We have many people to thank for their contributions to this book. The following individuals assisted us in a variety of ways and we are grateful for their help:

E-TEAMS Advisory Board

Shari L. Britner, associate professor of teacher education, Bradley University

Kevin Gannon, science department chair, Geneva High School

Shawn M. Glynn, Josiah Meigs Distinguished Teaching Professor, Educational Psychology Department and Mathematics & Science Education Department, University of Georgia

Kenneth King, professor of science education, Roosevelt University

Isabelle Y. Kovarik, science department chair and teacher, DeKalb High School

Jon S. Miller, professor of biology, Northern Illinois University

Steve Stern, science teacher, West Aurora High School

Ad Hoc Reviewers

Eduardo Briceño, Mindset Works

Hayal Kackar-Cam, postdoctoral research fellow, Northern Illinois University

Deborah Kalkman, instructor of educational psychology, Northern Illinois University

Jean Pierce, emeritus professor of educational psychology, Northern Illinois University

Corwin Press Reviewers

Jessica Allan, Corwin editor

Randy Cook, science teacher, Howard City, MI

Mandy Frantti, science teacher, Munising, MI\

Patti Grammens, science teacher, Cumming, GA

Jane Hunn, science teacher, Akron, IN

Debra K. Las, science teacher, Rochester, MN

Debra Meyer, series coeditor, professor of education, Elmhurst College, IL

Jeanine Nakakura, STEM resource teacher, Honolulu, HI

For Assistance With Preparing the Book and Accompanying Materials

Anna Collins, graduate student assistant, Northern Illinois University

Neil Colwell, web designer, Northern Illinois University

Nancy Defrates-Densch, instructor of educational psychology, Northern Illinois University

Jan DeVore, staff, Northern Illinois University

Pavielle Dortch, summer assistant, Northern Illinois University

Deborah Kalkman, instructor of educational psychology, Northern Illinois University

Janelle Grzetich, teacher, Minooka High School

Jen Howard, videographer, Northern Illinois University Media Services

Derek Johnson, video intern, Northern Illinois University

Dan Kapper, video intern, Northern Illinois University

Diane Layng, graphic artist, College Relations, Northern Illinois University

Nina Mounts, director, Collaborative on Early Adolescence, Northern Illinois University

Matt Ropp, video intern, Northern Illinois University

Marc VanOverbeke, acting department chair and associate professor, Northern Illinois University

Diana Zaleski, graduate student assistant, Northern Illinois University

The Scientists, Teachers, and Students who graciously allowed us to film them

SciMo Team and Participants

M Cecil Smith (co-principal investigator)

Brett Anderson

Anne Darfler

Nancy Defrates-Densch

Brian Gerber

Nigora Hamidova

Hayal Kackar-Cam

Deborah Kalkman

Elena Lyutykh

Solanlly Ochoa-Angrino

Anna Strati

Jay Thomas

Diana Zaleski

Teachers and Students who graciously allowed us to study them

National Science Foundation

Jolene Jesse, program officer for SciMo and E-TEAMS

Evaluator

Penny Billman, REGS Consulting LLC

About the Authors

Lee Shumow is distinguished teaching professor of educational psychology at Northern Illinois University. She teaches graduate-level courses in adolescent development, family and community partnerships, and research methodology in learning environments as well as undergraduate courses for preservice teachers. She began her career as a classroom teacher and is dedicated to preparing preservice teachers for middle school and secondary school teaching. Her recent research has been dedicated to understanding the role of families and teachers in fostering adolescents' school success.

Jennifer A. Schmidt is associate professor of educational psychology at Northern Illinois University. She teaches graduate-level classes in academic motivation and research design and is involved in the undergraduate teacher education program. She has conducted research in dozens of middle schools and high schools across the United States. For the past six years, she has had the privilege of visiting middle and high school science classrooms to study gender and motivation in science.

We dedicate this book to our parents, husbands, and children and to the teachers and students who inspired this book.

CHAPTER ONE

Introduction

Motivation to Learn Science

At a very basic level, motivation (the drive to pursue, work toward, and accomplish a goal) can be described as either *intrinsic* or *extrinsic*. *Intrinsic motivation* refers to the internal psychological impetus an individual has to pursue and fulfill a particular goal because it is enjoyable, interesting, fulfilling, or meaningful to the person. *Extrinsic motivation*, on the other hand, refers to impetus that comes from outside an individual in the form of giving or withholding tangible rewards (grades, points, approval, praise, special privileges, or goods) or meting out punishments (demerits, detentions, chastisement). From these definitions, it can be seen that motivation is situational—it varies depending on the goal and characteristics of the environment. Motivation is a state, not a trait.

We focus on intrinsic motivation to learn in this book for several reasons. The first reason is practical: In reality, both extrinsic and intrinsic motivations play a role in sparking learning, but most schools already capitalize heavily on extrinsic motivation. As a result, teachers have been exposed to and have access to many techniques that attempt to promote learning through the use of external means, such as reinforcements or punishments. Most teachers have far less exposure to knowledge and strategies for fostering intrinsic motivation. The second reason is theoretical: Every major contemporary theory of motivation considers

1

intrinsic motivation central to how deeply and how well students learn. The empirical research, our third reason, has provided considerable support for the idea that intrinsic motivation is key to sustained learning.

This book fills a gap in the science education literature by identifying motivational and affective processes involved in science learning, by illuminating experiential differences (and thus differential educational needs), and by focusing on practical ways to apply the information. This knowledge is valuable only if it gets in your hands. After all, you are likely to be your students' primary source of exposure to science. To supplement this book, we have created the E-TEAMS website (http://www.niu.edu/eteams), which will provide you with video demonstrations, ancillary materials, additional resources, and links.

THE SciMo PROJECT

For the past several years, our research team has had the opportunity to gather extensive data on students' experiences in high school science classrooms. We have amassed hundreds of hours of classroom video and observations in science classrooms of all levels, have spoken to science teachers, and have gathered information about how male and female students feel when they are doing various science activities. We will draw upon this research extensively throughout the book to illustrate students' experiences in science and demonstrate various motivational constructs. Although there seems to be broad agreement among science teachers that motivation to learn science is a critical factor in student success, there have been few studies of motivation within high school science classrooms. Therefore, although other relevant studies will be cited, many of the research results described in the text will come from a study we conducted with M Cecil Smith called the Science-in-the-Moment (SciMo) Project, which was funded by the National Science Foundation.[1] The SciMo Project documented the daily experiences and activities of male and female students in high school science courses. The methodology for the study is summarized in an appendix at the end of this book so that interested readers can learn about it in more detail.

---

[1] Award number HRD-0927526

HOW TIME WAS USED IN CLASSROOMS

Activities During Science Class

One of the most basic ways that we described the classrooms we studied in the SciMo Project was by the type of activity that was going on during science classes. Figure 1.1 shows the proportion of time spent in various activities. In their 50-minute class periods, seatwork took up more time than any other single activity. However, altogether, teachers spent an average of 56 minutes per week (24 percent of their total classroom time) on activities other than instruction, mostly in noninstructional management (38 minutes per week) and less often in off-task activities (18 minutes per week). Lab and testing, including

Figure 1.1 How Science Teachers Spend Their Classroom Time

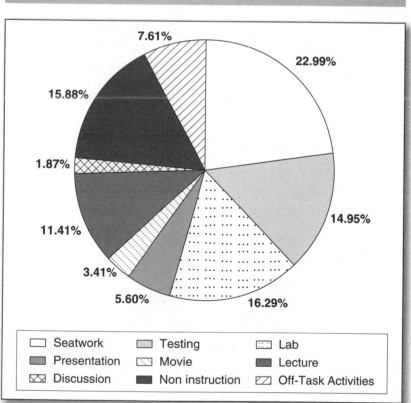

reviewing and going over tests, were also relatively common. Lecture accounted for slightly more than twice as much time as student presentations. Watching movies and class discussion were relatively uncommon. It is important to note that there were considerable differences between teachers in how time was allocated for different activities.

Teacher Talk During Science Class

In a 50-minute class period, teachers talked 27 minutes, on average. Most teacher talk addressed the whole class and was predominately teacher initiated. As shown in Figure 1.2, teachers talked most in order to move the lesson along, directing students about how to complete their work. They focused on science content knowledge (declarative science knowledge) far less often. Little time was spent focusing on elaboration of content (explanation of why and how) and teacher talk that fostered thinking amounted to

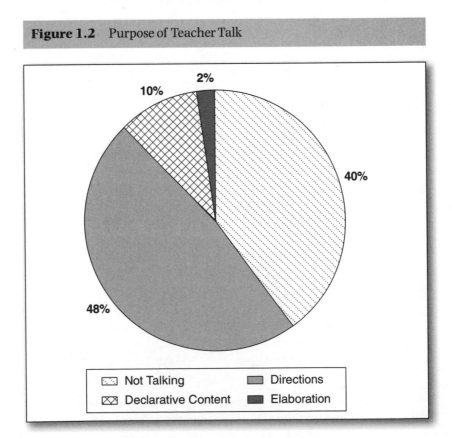

Figure 1.2   Purpose of Teacher Talk

2%
10%
40%
48%

Not Talking   Directions
Declarative Content   Elaboration

less than 1 minute of class time per week on average across all classes. In terms of whom the teachers talked to, about 56 percent of teachers' total talk time was spent addressing the whole class (about 15 minutes per class period), with the remaining 12 minutes per class period spent addressing individual students or small groups of students.

THE STUDENT PERSPECTIVE ON HIGH SCHOOL SCIENCE CLASSES

These days, both researchers and teachers agree that it is important to understand the students' perspective in order to be an effective teacher (Dall'Alba & Sandberg, 2006; Daniels & Shumow, 2003; Zhang, Koehler, Lundeberg, Eberhardt, & Parker, 2010). However, most science teacher education programs and professional development programs have not paid much attention to helping teachers to understand their students' perspectives or motivation. This book answers science teachers' need for that information.

Our research in science classes provides a unique opportunity to access students' perspectives on their classroom experience as they are engaged in learning activities. We asked students to carry small vibrating pagers during their science lessons for several days at different points during the school year. Using a remote transmitter, we signaled students at random moments in class. This signal prompted the students to fill out a very brief questionnaire in which they reported their thoughts and feelings. This unique method of data collection, called the Experience Sampling Method (ESM), provided repeated snapshots of students' experience in science and allowed us to understand what students were thinking and feeling in different classroom circumstances (for a comprehensive review of ESM methodology, see Hektner, Schmidt, & Csikszentmihalyi, 2007). We gathered more than 4,000 reports from the students in our study. Because motivational processes are internal, it is often difficult for teachers to assess them by simply observing students, so the ESM affords a unique window into student experience.

We learned that students enjoyed science class "a little" and thought that what they were doing had little relationship to their future goals. They reported very little stress, low challenge, and very little excitement. The students reported feeling somewhat skilled. While students almost always reported being engaged in some kind of science activity when they were signaled, their thoughts were not always on science. Students told us that they were thinking about science-related things in about 40 percent of their responses to the ESM signals. The remainder of the time, they indicated they were thinking about other things, such as plans for later in the day, lunch time, friends, and romantic interests.

Students' motivation and engagement varied by the activities that they were doing when they were signaled and by their teachers' verbal interaction patterns with them. We found a paradox in that the learning activities that students saw as more enjoyable were relatively unimportant to them, and the less enjoyable activities were viewed as more important. Students' emotions during specific class activities are discussed in greater detail in Chapter 10. Teachers varied widely in the nature and length of their interactions with students. These interaction patterns were also associated with students' learning and motivational outcomes to varying degrees. Specific details about teachers' interaction patterns with students are presented throughout the book.

GENDER DIFFERENCES IN STUDENT MOTIVATION AND PERSPECTIVE

Gender is a theme throughout this book, but the book is not just about female students. Overall, engagement in science class was low for both boys and girls and can be enhanced for both. Therefore, some findings we will present and strategies we will recommend apply equally to boys and girls, while others are specific to one gender or the other.

Before reading on, please stop for a moment and consider the following thought experiment. This was something we did with the teachers in our study and have also done with teachers in professional development settings. Those teachers told us that this was a very enlightening exercise.

Thought Experiment

First, consider what you believe about male and female students. Do you think that there are gender differences in performance, ability, enjoyment, interest, or participation in science?

Second, follow these directions in order to complete the chart displayed in Figure 1.3: Think of one (or each one) of your science classes. Identify your highest-achieving male student in the class and your highest-achieving female student in the class. Write the boy's name in the top left box and the girl's name in the top right box. Then think about a male student and a female student who really struggle in your class. Write the boy's name in the bottom left box and the girl's name in the bottom right box. Jot down a few words that characterize each student. Now, think about and list how the two students in each row are alike and how they are different. Next, compare and contrast the pair of students in each column.

How did you characterize your high-achieving students? Did you think of them as hard workers, curious, naturally gifted, or talented? How about the struggling students? How did you characterize the male compared to the female students?

Figure 1.3 Thought Experiment: Gender and Science Achievement

Highest-achieving Male Student

> Name:
>
> Characteristics:

Highest-achieving Female Student

> Name:
>
> Characteristics:

Lowest-achieving Male Student

> Name:
>
> Characteristics:

Lowest-achieving Female Student

> Name:
>
> Characteristics:

Our investigation of teachers' beliefs about gender and science revealed that few teachers explicitly identified gender differences in terms of ability, interest, or future potential in science. However, implicit beliefs were revealed in their descriptions of highest-achieving students—both male and female teachers described their high-achieving male students as having greater natural ability and their high-achieving female students as being harder workers with less curiosity and ability than their male classmates. Teachers in the SciMo study also predicted that more male students were likely to have a future in science than female students.

Teachers' implicit gendered beliefs about curiosity and ability were inconsistent with other data we had gathered that more directly assessed students' curiosity and ability. For example, when we looked at boys' and girls' own reports of interest during science, there were very few differences by gender across the different classroom activities. Likewise, when we examined students' grades in science (an imperfect indicator of ability), few gender differences emerged, and when they did, they suggested that girls were performing better than boys.

THE EXPERIENCE OF BOYS AND GIRLS IN SCIENCE

Recently, the gender gap in science has fallen off the radar screen of most teachers, possibly because many teachers believe that the long-standing historic gender gap has been addressed and possibly because girls have been achieving as well as boys in high school science courses (Sadker, Sadker, & Zittleman, 2009; Sanders, 2010). Nevertheless, girls choose to study science less often than boys when they get to college, suggesting that the situation for many female students might be "I can do it, I just don't want to." Our data illuminated systematic gender differences in the lived experience of students in science class, both in terms of students' internal reactions to specific learning situations and in the quality of their daily interactions with their science teachers.

The data we gathered with the ESM allowed us to compare the way that boys and girls feel in science class by looking at their momentary reports of enjoyment, stress, skill, and the like. Our data suggest that science may hold similar potential for engaging boys and girls but that this potential is not currently being realized equally for boys and girls. Figure 1.4 shows that boys and girls report similar levels of interest, importance, and hard work in science class. To us, this is hopeful: Boys and girls seem to equally value the activities they are doing in science class and are making similar levels of investment in their daily science activities. However, when we turn to other dimensions of students' lived experience in science, boys and girls start to look very different from one another. On a daily basis, girls report feeling significantly more frustrated and less skilled relative to their male peers. They are also less happy in science class.

Figure 1.4 How Boys and Girls Feel in Science Class

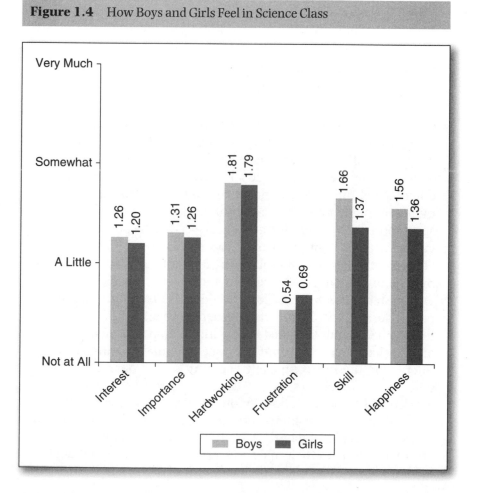

As you will read in the chapters that follow, several cognitive and affective factors presumed to be critical motivational processes (e.g., challenge, relevance, goal orientation, ability beliefs) operated differently for male students compared to female students in the SciMo study and suggest a motivational disadvantage for girls (Schmidt, Kackar, & Strati, 2010). The particular combination of experiential differences we documented in our study suggests that even though girls are performing as well as boys in science and share similar levels of interest in classroom activities, the actual sentiment among many girls is "I cannot do it, and I don't want to." This finding suggests that science teachers may do well to put gender back on their radar screens, despite apparent gender parity in science course-taking and achievement.

GENDER AND TEACHER-STUDENT INTERACTION

Our analysis of classroom video data revealed subtle but quantifiable bias against girls. Science teachers spent 39 percent more class time talking to their male students than their female students (Shumow & Schmidt, 2013). While this figure represents a difference of only a few minutes per day, it adds up to nearly 40 more minutes per month—nearly an entire class period. Teachers spent more time addressing boys than girls for the purpose of conveying basic content (43 percent more), moving the lesson along (17 percent more), elaborating on content (28 percent more), managing behavior (102 percent more), and discussing irrelevant material (92 percent more). Male students initiated a greater proportion of verbal interaction; teachers spent about 27 percent more time in male-initiated verbal interaction than female-initiated verbal interaction, but the fact that males initiated more interaction did not completely account for the observed gender differences in teachers' talk patterns with their students. There was considerable variation among teachers in these patterns, suggesting that these interaction patterns are not inevitable and can be changed. Notably, the variation we observed in how teachers interacted with their male and female students did not appear to be systematically related to teacher gender.

THE IMPORTANCE OF PROMOTING GENDER EQUITY IN SCIENCE

The inequities we documented are likely to have important implications for students. For one, an inequitable environment is likely to impact a student's perceptions of his or her own and others' abilities in science. Girls may come to doubt their abilities and boys might come to inflate their own abilities in response to unequal attention from teachers during science class. Girls might receive the message that they are valued only for their compliance to rules, while boys might take away the message that they are bad students. Further, both boys and girls may come to devalue the role and possible contributions of women in science, leading to continued gender bias in upper-level science classes and science careers.

Secondly, teachers' expectations of and interaction patterns with students have been implicated repeatedly in the development of long-term interest and persistence in science, technology, engineering, and mathematics (STEM) fields. Unless something changes, we predict that teachers will continue to espouse the implicit belief, which is not reflective of reality, that high school boys are more curious and better equipped to succeed in science than girls. The likely result is that we will continue to see gender gaps in science interest and persistence beyond high school in the United States (see Hill, Corbett, & St. Rose, 2010, for a review).

Finally, facility in scientific knowledge is essential for the future success of both individuals and societies. In our complex technological world, scientific literacy is important in many facets of life, including home, career, and citizenship. Scientific literacy will be enhanced to the extent that students are motivated to learn science. It is wise (and just) for educators to foster the potential and development of all students in scientific literacy. Increasing student motivation to learn is a crucial step and can be achieved!

WHAT RESOURCES CAN SCIENCE TEACHERS USE TO GET MORE BACKGROUND INFORMATION?

The companion website, http://www.niu.edu/eteams, contains helpful resources for teachers to use to learn more about the background information presented here. The following and more can be found on the website:

- Links to detailed information about the methodology of the SciMo Project as well as papers, publications, and reports that were produced from this project, including a paper about parent involvement in science
- Some general information about motivation to learn science
- Resources to better understand current gender gaps in interest and persistence in science

CHAPTER TWO

Value

"This is so boring," complains Marcie as she works on the homework problems pertaining to velocity and acceleration of model cars that her lab group tested in physics class. *"I'm going to be a doctor. I have an important exam in anatomy tomorrow; I need to be studying for it—not doing this. But if I blow it off and get an A- in physics, that could mean I won't graduate in the top 5 percent and that's just not who I am. I wonder whatever possessed me to listen to my guidance counselor about how valuable this stupid physics class would be. Maybe I can get the answers from Sam. He actually thinks this stuff is interesting. Not me, I don't care about cars."*

WHAT DOES IT MEAN TO VALUE SCIENCE?

Intrinsic Value

Students can value learning science or achieving in science class for a variety of different reasons. Perhaps they value learning science for its intrinsic value—because they are interested in it or because they enjoy it. Interest, one aspect of valuing, is a cognitive and emotional reaction to a subject or topic, characterized by attention, engagement, and positive feeling (Hidi & Renninger, 2006). Theorists believe that an inclination to seek and be interested in information is hardwired into people, based on neuroscientific evidence (Hidi, 2006; Renninger & Hidi, 2011).

In other words, our brain is structured to be interested in things. Our interest can take two different forms: situational interest and individual interest.

Situational interest describes what is happening when students say something like "Wow, that's really cool," in response to seeing or learning something new. It is a temporary response to something that is out of the ordinary, relevant to important aspects of their life, or emotionally compelling and is often generated because something or someone (a teacher or parent, for example) calls attention to or makes a connection to something relevant to the student (Renninger, 1992; Schiefele, 2009). *Individual interest* is thought to develop from situational interest over time and is enduring and stable (Hidi & Renninger, 2006; Schiefele, 2009). Once it has become well-developed, individual interest can be self-generated and maintained: There is no longer a need for someone else to make it interesting. To illustrate this progression from situational to individual interest, let us consider the development of Sam's interest in cars, which was referenced at the end of the vignette that opened this chapter. When Sam was six, his father took him to an auto race. Sam was mesmerized by the sounds, colors, and speed of all of the race cars: It was like nothing he had experienced before. His interest was triggered by the novelty of this situation. Sam's father supported his son's newfound situational interest, buying him toy race cars and taking him to an auto repair shop owned by a distant relative. As a result of this encouragement, Sam's interest deepened. When Sam was old enough to get a part-time job, he sought a position at a local auto parts store. He checked out books from the library and was a regular reader of several blogs about cars and auto racing. Sam's interest had now shifted to individual interest: It was no longer dependent on experiences provided by others. That interest led him to pay special attention in physics when they covered speed and velocity.

Utility Value

Students also might think that science is valuable, because knowing science or doing well in class will be useful for them in achieving a personal goal. Some students believe that learning science content is directly useful to them in the future (an idea called *utility value*). There are a number of different ways science can be perceived as useful, including for

- a future career or job;
- health, safety, or well-being;
- understanding routine events or popular culture;
- understanding of natural phenomena or problems that affect the individual or his or her loved ones;
- improving in sports or hobbies;
- learning other things he or she needs to know; or
- understanding or facilitating social relationships.

Attainment Value

Students might value knowing science or doing well in class for its attainment value—because it fits well with their idea of who they are, whether that vision consists of being a good student, a mem-

Used with permission of the National Science Teachers Association. Endorsement of this book is not implied.

ber of an analytic family, an altruist such as Albert Schweitzer, or a ground-breaking pioneer such as Marie Curie. Marcie, who is motivated to preserve her identity as a good student and who perceives herself as a helper, is motivated to some extent by what she can attain by learning.

Cost Value

On the other hand, students might value achievement in science because their investment in doing well in science will pay off relative to the alternatives (either the negative consequences of doing poorly or the lesser merits of succeeding at other endeavors that they could engage in instead). Students also often calculate the cost value of learning or achieving by deciding how much they will either gain or lose by taking a class, studying, or pursuing a goal. For example, in the vignette that opened this chapter, Marcie is considering whether doing her physics homework will cost her a good grade on her anatomy exam. She is also weighing the cost of not doing her physics homework to her goal to be at the top of her class. Cost value also entails an assessment of the emotional consequences of learning and doing well—whether it is exciting, frustrating, enjoyable, or stressful.

WHY IS VALUING SCIENCE IMPORTANT?

As a science teacher, you have most likely recognized that students who value science are considerably more motivated to learn science than students who do not see much value in it. You have probably recognized that many high school students do not perceive science as valuable for them outside of your classroom. The good news is that there are a number of well-established ways (described subsequently) to motivate your students by helping them to see how science is valuable for them.

Science Interest Declines With Age

High school students report less general interest in science than younger students and consequently tend to be less motivated to learn science in high school than they were in elementary school (Barmby, Kind, & Jones, 2008; George, 2000; Gottfried, Fleming, & Gottfried, 2001). This is a rather serious situation, because interest tends to engage students in what they are learning (Renninger & Hidi, 2011) and often results in students using deep rather than surface learning strategies (Wigfield & Eccles, 2000). Not surprisingly, then, interest also predicts subject area learning and competence (Schiefele, 2009).

Perceiving That Relevance Matters

Seeing science as relevant is a strong indicator of whether students will value science, become engaged in it, and persist in it (Koballa & Glynn, 2007). The more relevant students think that their classwork is, the more they see studying as a way to achieve their own goals and the more likely they will be to make the choice to engage in and study science as a result. Students who value science for its usefulness (utility value) are more likely to take science classes than those who do not think science is valuable for them (James, 2002).

Science Value Can Be
Connected to Students' Identity

Identity development is a central task of adolescence, so high school students are attuned to the potential attainment value inherent in science (Hofer, 2010). *Identity development* entails exploring career options as well as exploring and deciding on political, spiritual, and core philosophical beliefs, all of which can be informed by scientific knowledge and practice. For example, many environmental issues have political, spiritual, and philosophical aspects; thus making commitments about how to live and how to solve problems in a way that is aligned with personal values can be enriched by an understanding of the science that undergirds these issues.

WHAT HAVE RESEARCHERS DISCOVERED ABOUT VALUING SCIENCE IN CLASSROOMS?

Students See Little Value in Science

Many adolescents in the United States express little individual interest in science and are consequently less likely than those with genuine interest to major in science or enter careers that involve or depend upon science (Ames, 1992; National Science Board, 2004). Yet, there is much that teachers and parents can do to support interest development. As we described earlier in this chapter, with repeated exposure and support, situational interest can be triggered and can develop into individual interest, which then acts as its own trigger to a continuing cycle of interest (Renninger & Hidi, 2011). Teachers and parents can play a major role in triggering situational interest and supporting student exploration and, eventually, individual interest in science.

Our use of the Experience Sampling Method (ESM) in the Science-in-the-Moment (SciMo) study allowed us to take multiple snapshots of how students valued science while they were in science class; we also used surveys at the beginning and end of the study to gauge individual interest and any changes in interest. In general, we found that students perceived very little excitement in their classes, suggesting that situational interest (and intrinsic value) was not being triggered. Students also reported that science activities were only "a little" valuable to them. Situational interest was lowest in chemistry class, followed by general science class. Students showed more situational interest in biology classes and reported the highest levels of situational interest in physics.

Teachers Could Do More to Promote the Value of Science

Consistent with students' reports that indicated little triggering of interest, we observed little teacher enthusiasm for either the content or subjects they were teaching. Teachers rarely conveyed excitement, pleasure, or passion, which are the hallmarks of teacher enthusiasm for subject matter (Kunter, Frenzel, Nagy, Baumert, & Pekrun, 2011) and a way to trigger student interest in a subject. For students without high personal interest or value in science, the continued lack of situational triggers to evoke their curiosity circumvents the possibility of developing sustained interest in science.

Our analysis of classroom video data revealed that teachers missed many opportunities to promote relevance. In many cases, teachers made few connections between the content under study and its value for anything outside of the next quiz, test, or grade. Our data suggest that the students picked up on this message. Students rated testing as the activity that had the highest "importance to you" relative to all other classroom activities (this finding is represented graphically in Figure 10.1). Although teachers planned hands-on activities and labs, there was little or no connection made between these activities and the scientific concepts they were studying or the utility value of the content. In keeping with the need for students to be learning in order to maintain situational interest, we found that situational interest was higher and that students were more intellectually engaged when content focus was high during class. Unfortunately, we documented widespread inefficiency in the use of time, which cut into time used to introduce or elaborate on content.

Parents Can Influence Their Children's Valuing of Science

We also found that the level of parental involvement at home, which was defined as monitoring science homework and setting rules and routines conducive to school success, predicted how much students valued what they did during science class. Parents both influenced and were influenced by student interest in science. Students' individual interest in science was associated with greater parent involvement at home and at school. Both individual interest and parental involvement at home predicted students' situational interest during class. Interestingly, students' reports of struggling in science did not predict greater parent involvement, as it often does with younger children. Many parents are aware that high school students need to be thinking about their postsecondary paths, and their supportiveness of an academic interest might be a response to that. Parents might think that students should be concentrating on subjects that interest them and in which they are successful and turning away from subjects in which they struggle. Thus at a certain point, subjects that fall outside of a student's area of interest might be seen by parents as being potentially costly in that they would take the student's attention away from the work that was really important (the reader is referred to our discussion of cost value earlier in this chapter).

Promoting Science Value May Be Especially Effective When Students Doubt Their Ability

There is some evidence that students' beliefs about their ability (see Chapter 8) in science work together with their beliefs about the value of science. It stands to reason that students must believe that they can have the ability to do science and that science applies to their life or to things they value in order for them to choose to explore and learn science deeply. In a study by Hulleman and Harackiewicz (2009), students either wrote about how what they were learning was valuable to them or about a topic unrelated to valuing content. Students who had low competence beliefs subsequently were more interested and did better in class if they had written about how content was valuable to them. The importance of the value students described did not matter—students who identified the content as having significant value (e.g., curing a life-threatening disease) did not do better than students who identified minor value (e.g., predicting the need for a raincoat). Having students generate their own value was what mattered in predicting improvement (Harackiewicz, 2010).

There Are Some Gender
Differences in Science Interest and Value

Some gender differences in interest were evident in our study. We found that boys and girls had nearly the same level of situational interest during science activities, except in lab (a relatively rare activity), which boys found more interesting than girls. Even though girls and boys reported similar levels of daily situational interest in science, girls had less developed individual interest in science as a subject and were, therefore, less interested in pursuing careers in science than boys. The distinction between situational interest and individual interest seems an important one to make when considering gender and science. The fact that boys and girls have the same level of situational interest in science is cause for some hope, because it suggests that with proper and equitable support for situational interest and curiosity, individual interest for science has an equal chance of developing for boys and girls.

Some research has concluded that girls find science to have less general value than boys do, particularly among young adolescents (Catsambis, 1995; Lee & Berkham, 1996). However, we found no gender differences in high school students' reports that science class was important to them or to their future (Schmidt, Zaleski, Shumow, Ochoa-Angrino, & Hamidova, 2011). This might be because female students recognize that taking and doing well in science classes is important for admission to college (Baker & Leary, 1995; Greenfield, 1996). Thus girls might have seen science as temporarily useful to fill a relatively short-term goal but, because of repeated lack of support for situational science interest, girls may have less well-developed individual interest in science. Consequently, the girls in the SciMo study were less likely than boys to indicate that they planned on pursuing a science college major or career.

HOW CAN TEACHERS FOSTER VALUE?

Utilize Individual Interest

Teachers have many opportunities to motivate their students by applying knowledge about individual and situational interest in their classrooms. It is important to understand your students' individual interests so that you can connect those interests to the science content that you teach whenever possible. The easiest way to learn about students' interest is by giving a brief initial survey to both your students and their parents (most of whom are very good informants about their children's interests). If those interests pertain directly to careers in the science that you teach, you may want to encourage those students and also suggest any opportunities for them to advance their skill and knowledge outside of class, such as through watching science shows on television, attending camps at nearby colleges or universities, or participating in special events at area museums. If a student's interests are not directly related to the science that you teach, connections can often still be made. Sometimes, interest inventories will give teachers ideas for examples to use in class. For instance, a physics teacher who has students who are passionately interested in technology, gaming, sports, music, and any number of other leisure pursuits can link numerous concepts in physics to those pastimes.

Foster Situational Interest

As an early stage in the development of interest, situational interest is typically externally generated and supported. Due to economic or time constraints, some students may have limited support for the development of interest at home. In these circumstances, it becomes even more critical for teachers to foster and support situational interest. Promoting relevance is the best of all strategies identified by experts for fostering situational interest and engaging students (Assor, Kaplan, & Roth, 2002). Utility value and attainment value also are bolstered when students think that the content is relevant to them personally. Two reviews of research on promoting relevance during instruction identified a number of techniques that teachers can use (Palmer, 2007; Schiefele, 2009). These reviews suggest the following techniques, also represented in Figure 2.1: (a) connect content to everyday life outside of class or other school subjects, (b) use everyday and well-known materials in labs and demonstrations, (c) model enthusiasm, (d) tell stories about how the topic mattered to specific people, (e) associate material being studied with individual students' interests, and (f) make analogies or metaphors to things that students understand (e.g., "It's like when you slam on the brakes in a car.").

Labs can easily be designed to demonstrate relevance (Robinson & Ochs, 2008). It is important to keep in mind that the relevance of the lab and the content needs to be made explicit through identification and discussion of the connections. We found that many of the teachers we observed thought that students would automatically make these connections, but that was not the case. Just because students tested the pH of common materials, for instance, they did not make the leap to knowing how pH levels might be relevant for them.

Use Available Resources to Promote Relevance

High school science teachers face some unique challenges in making content relevant, because doing so can require a deep

Figure 2.1   Techniques for Promoting Relevance

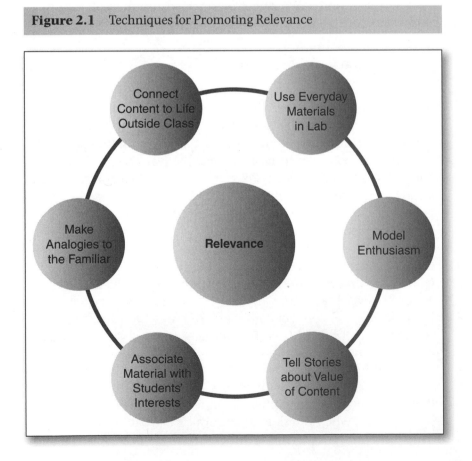

understanding of multiple specific topics, and high school teachers are required to teach a broad range of content in high school, making it almost impossible to have a deep understanding of all the topics in the common core and the latest science standards. One way to approach this challenge is to use resources such as those recommended on the companion website. Another way is to get advice from practicing scientists while planning. Numerous projects have connected teachers with scientists, but those have tended to entail either presentations or internships. A partnership centered on planning has the advantages of using the experience and expertise of both the scientist and the teacher, and it can be done asynchronously (through e-mail, for example). Many scientists care about science education and work for companies or organizations willing to support regional schools and the development of young scientists. In our experience, teachers who call upon scientists for this purpose have found them to be very receptive. A guide for finding scientists is included in the resources we provide on the website.

Have Students Reflect on the Value of What They Are Learning

Teachers also can help students to realize how the content is meaningful to their lives by asking students to make those connections by writing about or discussing the topic (Hulleman & Harackiewicz, 2009). As noted in the research review presented earlier in this chapter, these student-generated connections can be quite motivating, even when they are relatively basic and simple. Teachers can ask students to suggest examples of the content in their own lives.

Use Problem-Based Learning

Yet another way to promote relevance, utility value, and attainment value is to associate science topics with societal issues and with decisions students must make as citizens. Problem-based learning (PBL) has been widely used by high school science teachers to promote achievement, scientific thinking, and student motivation (Savery & Duffy, 1996). PBL involves ill-structured or messy problems that don't have clear solutions or single correct answers: The point of the exercise is to build problem-solving skills in a content area with real-world situations. The situations you select to mirror real-world problems can be situated in your communities and/or be attuned to culturally or socially relevant issues that are meaningful to your students. See the companion website for PBL resources.

Maintain Enthusiasm

Enthusiasm is extremely important in generating student interest in a subject or topic. As teachers ourselves, we find it useful to consciously focus on what initially captivated us about our subjects when we are preparing to teach our students. Keeping abreast of new developments and learning new things also helps us to maintain our enthusiasm for topics we teach repeatedly.

Use Storytelling

Some teachers have found that storytelling is a good way to foster the value of content for their students by "humanizing" it (Darby-Hobbs, 2011). The stories might come from their own experience working as or with scientists or from their daily life. Stories also can be drawn from current events or from biographical or historical information about famous scientists. For example, while attending mass, Galileo timed the period of a swaying chandelier and noticed that the period never changed despite the diminishing amplitude as the chandelier slowly came to rest. The seemingly inconsequential event was profoundly inspirational to his nascent scientific career. Many students may have also felt bored in a church service and can relate to Galileo. See the companion website for storytelling resources.

Develop Culturally Relevant Activities

As classrooms become more culturally diverse, many science teachers wonder how to adjust their teaching to ensure students of diverse backgrounds find their classes relevant. A paper by Boutte, Kelly-Jackson, and Johnson (2010) provides examples of how several science lessons taught typical scientific concepts using activities that were aligned with students' backgrounds. For example, one class of predominately African American students studied and presented reports on diseases such as sickle cell anemia. An environmental science teacher we know who has many Mexican-American students has her students study environmental issues in Mexico and Central America.

Involve Families

Given parents' influence on whether and how students value science, teachers can include families in several ways. As noted previously, teachers can survey parents about their children's interests. Teachers can encourage and support parents in fostering their children's interests in science: Pertinent television shows, documentaries, museum exhibits or programs, and university science programs can be posted on teachers' webpages and e-mail reminders about those opportunities could be sent. Teachers can inform parents of upcoming celestial events, such as full moons, lunar eclipses, or meteor showers. Note that many of these opportunities for parents to support their child's interest can be free or low-cost. As described in Chapter 3, teachers also can facilitate parents' positive influence at home by providing tips about homework and by assigning homework that involves discussion of current societal issues related to science content. Finally, parents can be encouraged to promote their children's postsecondary and career exploration when teachers acknowledge the influence of parents and connect parents to resources about career exploration. These small steps can be especially important for parents who did not attend college.

WHAT RESOURCES CAN SCIENCE TEACHERS USE TO PROMOTE VALUE?

The companion website, http://www.niu.edu/eteams, contains helpful resources for teachers to use to promote value of science in their classrooms or to recommend for parents of their students. The following and more can be found on the website:

- Interest surveys to give students
- Links to materials and lesson plans promoting utility value of high school science topics

- Storytelling resources
- Guides for finding practicing scientists to elaborate on the value of particular science content
- Problem Based Learning (PBL) resources
- Links about science careers
- Streaming video clips exemplifying practices recommended in this chapter
- Streaming video clips of scientists discussing how adults helped them understand the value of science and of science teachers exemplifying the practices recommended in this chapter

CHAPTER THREE

Affiliation

On a crisp fall afternoon after school, a middle-aged high school physics teacher sat in the school courtyard engrossed in conversation with two of his students, worksheets strewn across the table, calculators in hand. From a distance, it was not at all obvious that this was a physics teacher helping his students—their body language indicated a comfort with one another similar to that often observed between people who have known one another for a long time. Together, they worked through some acceleration homework problems. As they discussed the problems, they were smiling, joking, and animated in a way that suggested deep engagement. The students finished and left, cheerfully saying, "See you tomorrow!" Several other groups of students—boys and girls—stopped at his table to say hello, making comments about something they enjoyed in class that day, clarifying what they needed to have ready for the following day, or even chatting about their extracurricular activities or siblings.

The ease with which this teacher interacted with his students indicates a positive, mutually satisfying relationship that serves as a powerful motivator for his students to learn science. As a practical guide for educators, this chapter focuses on how a teacher can build such positive student-teacher relationships, establish a positive classroom climate, and nurture positive peer interactions around science.

WHAT DO CLASSROOM SOCIAL RELATIONSHIPS INCLUDE IN HIGH SCHOOL?

There is no single picture of positive relationships in the context of a high school classroom. Nevertheless, some key ingredients can be described so that individual teachers can find a way of expressing and enacting these relationships in a way that fits each teacher's individual style, personality, and circumstances. At the most basic level, the teacher-student relationship is built on the level of care and support communicated to students. Most scholars today believe that support takes several different forms, including emotional support, instrumental support, inclusion of students' perspectives, and positive classroom climate (Pianta, 1999; Wentzel, Battle, Russell, & Looney, 2010).

Emotional Support

Emotional support is also called *teacher sensitivity* by some. It entails anticipating and responding to students' concerns and needs in the classroom, being dependable and consistent, and demonstrating interest in and sensitivity to students' lives outside of the classroom (Stuhlman, Hamre, Downer, & Pianta, 2012).

Attention to Student Perspectives

Having regard for students' perspectives also plays a role in the quality of the teacher-student relationship. This includes communicating that each student is a valuable contributor to the classroom learning community; incorporating students' interests, goals, and perspectives into class activities and discussions; providing students some choice and control (see Chapter 4); and encouraging all students to participate and contribute in class (Stuhlman et al., 2012). Attending to student perspectives allows science teachers to understand students' misconceptions and provides them with access to information they can draw on for examples that will pique students' interests and values (see Chapter 2).

Instrumental Support

Teachers can also provide what some have called *instrumental support* to students. This includes attending to individual students' learning needs, creating learning environments that support these individual differences, and providing the resources and assistance that are necessary for students to effectively complete their academic work (Patrick, Anderman, & Ryan, 2002; Strati, 2011). Wentzel (1997) found that young adolescent students defined a teacher who cares as one who wants to help them to learn and do well in class. In other words, students characterized teachers who provide instrumental support as caring.

Positive Classroom Climate

Classroom climate describes the general mood of a classroom. A positive climate is found in classrooms where there is a sense of psychological safety, where teachers and students enjoy being together and are respectful of one another, and where the parties are enthusiastic about learning together. A positive climate is also characterized by the absence of a negative environment in which irritation, anger, hostility, negative interactions, belittling, and teasing frequently occur (Stuhlman et al., 2012).

Positive Peer Relationships

It is beyond the scope of this chapter to examine the many ways that peers influence adolescents' behaviors, attitudes, and aspirations through friendships, peer crowds, cliques, and romantic relationships. Our focus is on peer relationships that further learning and motivation in a classroom. In science, that includes working in small groups, working with lab partners, and participating in discussions. The skills necessary to engage in these activities include listening to, responding to, explaining, helping, and accommodating the ideas of

Wavebreakmedia Shutterstock

others; contributing and following through on tasks and roles; and working toward and monitoring progress toward a shared goal.

WHY ARE CLASSROOM SOCIAL RELATIONSHIPS IMPORTANT?

A Basic Need

Conventional wisdom has it that teenagers are motivated to come to school for the social relationships they have there, not the education they receive. Many mistakenly assume that those relationships are limited to peers. However, high school students also find their relationships with their teachers important. Several motivation theories suggest that humans have a basic need for affiliation, relatedness, or belongingness that underlies much of their behavior (Deci & Ryan, 1985, 1991; Goodenow, 1993; Murray, 1938). In school settings, this basic need is fulfilled by both teachers and peers.

Relationships Contribute to Student Performance

The classroom social environment plays a critical role in shaping students' academic, behavioral, and motivational outcomes (Allen et al., 2012; Burnett, 2002; Midgley, Feldlaufer, & Eccles, 1989; Patrick et al., 2002; Wentzel, 2002). Peer relationships in classrooms also influence students' learning and motivation in high school.

Scientific Progress Depends on Collaboration

Importantly, science is fundamentally collaborative. Scientific progress depends on teamwork and peer interaction. Past and current science standards have emphasized teaching students about the nature of science and introducing them to the work of scientists. Collaboration is a lifelong skill that students can learn in science class that will benefit them in their future, no matter what course they pursue.

High-School Structure Can Undermine Relationships

Some researchers have suggested that poor student-teacher relationships are almost inevitable, given the structure of American high schools, and that these poor relationships may contribute to the general difficulties that many students experience during adolescence. High schools are typically larger, more bureaucratic, and more impersonal than middle schools, and high school students tend to move around more and spend less "face time" with their teachers (Anderman & Anderman, 2010; Dornbusch & Kaufman, 2001; Eccles et al., 1993). This aspect of the typical American high school makes it especially important for teachers to focus on developing positive relationships with their students.

Teachers Can Facilitate Positive Relationships

As leaders in their classroom, teachers have tremendous power to influence the types of relationships that develop there. Teachers' relationships with students, peer relationships among students in the class, and general classroom climate can have profound impacts on students' learning and engagement, even in high schools, which are often designed in a way that makes building such relationships challenging. While we were filming the video clips of exemplary teachers for our companion website, we repeatedly saw and heard examples of how important it was to the students that their teacher facilitated positive relationships.

Teachers play a critical role supporting students' need to feel connected in the school context. High school students spend a substantial amount of time in school with their teachers—more time, in many cases, than they spend with their own parents. It stands to reason that positive relationships with teachers can further support positive adult-child relationships many students experience at home and may even compensate for home relationships that are less than supportive.

WHAT HAVE RESEARCHERS DISCOVERED ABOUT CLASSROOM RELATIONSHIPS IN SCIENCE?

Establishing Meaningful Student-Teacher Relationships in High School Is Hard

Eccles and her colleagues (1993) reported that teachers in the larger and more bureaucratic high school environment were perceived by students as less warm and more controlling relative to teachers in smaller schools at lower grade levels. Add to this the natural developmental progression for adolescents to seek more autonomy and independence, and students and teachers in the modern high school can be like two ships that pass in the night. This phenomenon is not unique to science teachers, but given the anxiety that many students feel about science in particular (refer to Chapter 10), positive student-teacher relationships in science may be especially critical. Anderman and Anderman (2010) have suggested that while the nature of the high school environment might make it more difficult to develop positive student-teacher relationships, it might also make these relationships more critical than ever: A caring and supportive teacher might be just what a student needs to navigate a challenging situation and thrive.

Girls May Be Particularly Responsive to Teacher Behaviors in STEM Subjects

Teachers are important role models for students' learning: They demonstrate and exemplify many of the skills that students are expected to learn in a course, and in many cases, they serve as models for specific careers or fields of study. Research on modeling indicates that we learn best from models who we respect and with whom we have positive relationships. Thus, when teachers have more positive relationships with their students, their students feel more confident and learn more. There is also some evidence that we learn best from models who we perceive as similar to us in some way (Bandura, 1986; Schunk, 1989). Thus there could be some particular benefit to female students developing positive relationships with women in science.

In their study of successful female scientists, Zeldin and Pajares (2000) found that all of the successful female scientists in their study credited a teacher (often a middle school or high school teacher) as being instrumental in the development of their competence and confidence. Specifically, these women scientists felt that they benefitted from the emotional and academic support they received from their teachers (both male and female) and described their teachers as being particularly committed to the success in science of their female students. It is notable that the women in this study also viewed some of their former teachers as obstacles that were eventually overcome. It appears that girls may be more responsive than boys to teacher behaviors and characteristics in science, technology, engineering, and mathematics (STEM) areas.

For example, from an early age, girls are more likely than boys to attribute both their successes and failures in math to the degree of help they get from teachers (Lloyd, Walsh, & Yailagh, 2005). As early as elementary school, studies show that when female teachers project math anxiety, over the course of the school year, this anxiety gets "handed down" to the girls in the class (but not to the boys) and negatively impacts girls' math achievement (Beilock, Gunderson, Ramirez, & Levine, 2010).

When Teachers Are Supportive, Students Are More Engaged in Math and Science

Students' perceptions of teacher support and general school belonging tend to decline as they move through adolescence (Sun & Hui, 2007). However, research suggests that perceiving teachers as supportive may be even more important for adolescents than it is for elementary students. When adolescents perceive their teachers as supportive, they are more engaged in school, whereas the relationship between perceived support and engagement is weaker for elementary students (Klem & Connell, 2004). In a study of the classroom and school learning climate in mathematics classes in more than 90 Canadian schools, Willms, Friesen, and Milton (2009) found that students were one and a half times more likely to be engaged in their classwork when their relationship with the teacher was positive. In our own research in high school physics classrooms, we found that when students perceived their science teachers as supportive, they were more engaged (Strati & Schmidt, 2012, 2013). Additionally, teacher support bolstered the positive effect of challenge on student engagement. In other words, as a general rule, challenge heightened student engagement; the addition of teacher support heightened it even further. Conversely, when teachers were sarcastic or threatening, even to a single student, the general engagement level of all students in the classroom declined (Strati & Schmidt, 2013).

Research suggests that positive relationships with teachers may enhance students' feelings of competence, which, in turn, has a positive influence on student learning and overall psychological health (Wentzel & Battle, 2001). Science, particularly at the more advanced levels, is often perceived as an intimidating subject. Girls tend to feel less competent relative to boys in science (Shumow & Schmidt, 2013). Given girls' lack of confidence in their scientific abilities and their heightened responsiveness to teacher characteristics and behaviors in STEM areas, the student-teacher relationship presents a ripe opportunity to influence girls' learning and engagement in science.

When Teachers Create a Positive Classroom Climate, Their Students Achieve More

In a study involving high school science and other subject areas, Allen et al. (2012) identified five specific aspects of teachers' classroom interactions that directly and dramatically improved student achievement over the course of a school year (see Figure 3.1). These aspects include (1) a classroom environment that reflects

Figure 3.1   Student-Teacher Interaction Dimensions That Foster Student Achievement

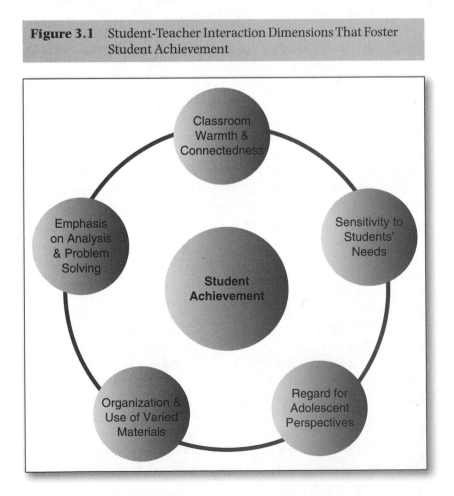

warmth and connectedness; (2) teacher sensitivity to students' emotional and academic needs; (3) teacher regard for adolescent perspectives, which includes recognition of students' need to be active and autonomous and attending to peer interaction in the classroom; (4) teacher organization and use of varied learning materials; and (5) teacher emphasis on higher-order thinking skills through analysis and problem-solving activities. Each of these factors independently raised student achievement over the course of a year, and when teachers did all five of these things well, student achievement gains were most dramatic. The lesson here is that teachers have a variety of avenues through which they can positively interact with students to enhance their achievement (Mikami, Gregory, Allen, Pianta, & Lun, 2011).

Peer Interaction in Science Deepens Scientific Knowledge and Remediates Scientific Misunderstandings

In one of their seminal publications, cooperative learning experts Johnson and Johnson (1987) suggested that one of the potential benefits of cooperative learning is that it may help students learn to be more scientific as they systematically test their own understandings against those of others. Indeed, research conducted in science classrooms suggests that facilitating positive peer interaction around scientific concepts aids in learning. For example, in randomized experimental studies involving ninth- and eleventh-grade science classrooms, students who were exposed to cooperative learning in chemistry had higher content knowledge after instruction than those exposed to traditional instruction (Acar & Tarhan, 2007, 2008). Cooperative learning was also more effective at remediating a number of common misunderstandings about electrochemistry relative to traditional instruction (Acar & Tarhan, 2007). In interviews, the student participants in this study said that working in groups "provided opportunities to listen to each other, share ideas, and form new friendships" (p. 365). Students also noted that it was important for the teacher to visit their group regularly to monitor and guide them, saying that their participation in the group's activity increased when the teacher interacted with them more often. This observation made by students underscores the important role of the teacher in facilitating productive peer interaction in science.

Supportive School Relationships Can Facilitate Students' Self-Identification as Scientists or Scientifically Literate Citizens

During daily life, adolescents move through many "cultures"—peers, school, classroom, family, extracurricular activities. These cultures influence students' perceptions of themselves and the world around them. Students negotiate their developing identities, including academic identities, on the basis of their relationships in these various cultural contexts. If relationships in several of these cultures are positive, set high expectations, and support scientific learning, then students will be more likely to identify with a science persona and, as a result of this stronger identification, will be more likely to be resilient when academic challenges arise. The more a student is supported in the development of a science persona, the more likely he or she will be to either persist in a science career or persist in his or her science studies to become a scientifically literate citizen (Aschbacher, Li, & Roth, 2010). These kinds of identity supports may be particularly important for the development of science identities among girls (Brickhouse, Lowery, & Schultz, 2000).

HOW CAN TEACHERS BUILD POSITIVE RELATIONSHIPS WITH AND AMONG THEIR STUDENTS?

Learn About Individual Students

The ability to provide emotional support depends, to a large extent, on knowing your students as individuals. This is a challenging but not insurmountable task in large comprehensive high schools. Teachers can use surveys to learn about their students during the first week of school. The companion website contains sample surveys that you can use as they are or adapt for your own use. One teacher we know hands out index cards to parents at Open House and asks them to tell her anything they think is important for her to know about their child. Another teacher sends a letter home with a parent survey on the back side. His students address and stuff the envelopes, which include a self-addressed return envelope to the teacher.

These strategies provide a wealth of information that teachers can use to get to know their students.

Make the Time to Quickly Connect With Each Student

In our extensive observations of science classrooms, we have been struck by the many different ways that science teachers interact with their students immediately before, during, and just after class. Those teachers who manage to briefly greet or acknowledge as many individual students as possible tend to be the teachers with the very best relationships with students. The transition between classes is a very busy time, and teachers have many competing demands for their attention, but taking a few seconds for each student can really pay off in terms of students' willingness to cooperate during class, because they feel cared for and respected by their teacher.

Bearing in mind the gender differences we observed in student-teacher interaction patterns (see Chapter 1), it is critically important for teachers to make these personal connections equally among their male and female students. In the classrooms we observed, it was inequities in this seemingly irrelevant talk that girls noticed most. There were several instances when one of the girls in a classroom would comment to us as researchers that a teacher was giving boys more attention than girls, but such comments were never made about course content: Instead, they universally referred to perceived inequities in greetings in hallways, comparison of notes about weekend sporting events, or friendly joking. Students notice when teachers do (and perhaps more importantly, do not) make these kinds of comments to them.

Follow Up If You Notice That Something Is Wrong

Sometimes simply asking a student if he or she is okay or if something is wrong is enough to communicate support. Other times, you might be able to help solve a school or class problem by providing information or a referral, because you know the system better than your students do. Yet other times, you can help by giving instrumental support on an assignment. What is most important is to avoid letting this follow-up get lost in the hustle and bustle of your day.

Solicit Students' Perspectives

Teachers can solicit students' perspectives by making sure that all students are expected to and do participate. This, too, is an area where we have observed substantial differences between teachers. Some teachers call almost exclusively on students who have volunteered, whereas others have established the expectation that all students will participate—they call on students or use techniques to make sure that everyone contributes. Some students are shy or hesitate to participate because of performance avoidance goals (see Chapter 7). Teachers can support those students by making sure that everyone has had a chance to prepare (and ask for help) before a class discussion or question-response activity.

The techniques described in Chapter 4 to provide choice and control fit well with incorporating the student perspective. It bears repeating that the student perspective is a fundamental aspect of the inquiry approach to science, and teachers are encouraged to use the many excellent resources available for honing those skills.

Provide Instrumental Support

Some of the science teachers we have observed closely monitor students and let them know how they are doing in class. If students are struggling, the teachers provide them with suggestions for improvement and offer opportunities for extra help (during lunch or after school) and post resources on the class webpage. One of the teachers we feature in the video clips on our website encourages students to study together, which has the added advantage of promoting peers as sources of academic support. Instrumental aid can also come in the form of having a student take notes that can be used by any students who were absent.

Establish a Positive Class Climate

Teachers set the general tone for the classroom social climate through their interactions with individual students and the class as a whole. When a teacher treats students with care, respect, and social responsiveness, then students are more likely to treat each other in the same way (Farmer, McAuliffe Lines, & Hamm, 2011). Humor that is not threatening or embarrassing to students can create a positive atmosphere, but not all teachers are comfortable using humor in the classroom—those teachers can foster enthusi-asm and enjoyment in other ways.

It is especially important to minimize hostility, sarcasm, or teasing by students or the teacher in the classroom. When that behavior occurs, it is often driven by social hierarchies. In planning for and setting up cooperative groups, you can use your knowledge of your students' social dynamics to your advantage and take care to avoid and respond to situations where a student may feel socially attacked. One way to do this is to set up clear rules and guidelines for group activities and to make sure that individuals are given tasks with clear goals to keep them focused (Farmer et al., 2011). Another is to carefully consider the social make up of groups when assigning group activities, being careful not to place particularly sensitive students in groups with students who are likely to tease or bully.

Plan to Make Group Work Successful

For group work to be successful, teachers need to plan carefully. This includes choosing the type of group structure to use for the task, assigning students to those groups, and identifying inter-dependent roles that students need to play within those groups (Johnson & Johnson, 1987). It also includes teaching students the skills for working together. Students need these skills to be identi-fied, modeled, practiced, and evaluated with feedback (Weinstein, 2003). One technique that we have found useful with high school students is the fishbowl. This entails having one group of students work together on a task while others watch and monitor the group functions. This technique has the advantage of continuing to focus on content while also processing collaborative skills. Finally, it is essential to plan for individual accountability in the process; ultimately, students need to be responsible for their own learning.

WHAT RESOURCES CAN SCIENCE TEACHERS USE TO UNDERSTAND AND BUILD POSITIVE RELATIONSHIPS?

The companion website, http://www.niu.edu/eteams, contains valuable resources to help teachers foster positive relationships in their classrooms or to recommend for parents of their students. The following and more can be found on the website:

- Surveys for getting to know your students better
- Links to websites with excellent briefs about fostering good teacher-student relationships
- Links to resources that offer student perspectives on how school relationships help them learn better
- Great articles with practical tips on making cooperative learning successful in the high school science classroom
- Streaming video clips showing examples of strong positive relationships in the high school science classroom

Chapter Four

Autonomy

> *"Whenever we're in Ms. Freeman's class, we're in charge. We have to direct it and make decisions. It's kind of cool. We never really get responsibility elsewhere, and later on in the workforce, it's going to be good that we had some experience with taking charge. When we're responsible for teaching the younger kids what we learned, it's more important and fun. Science was so boring the first couple of years of high school. I think I actually like science now, and I can't believe I'm hearing myself say that." Alysha, 11th-Grade Student*

WHAT IS AUTONOMY?

Autonomy is generally thought of as synonymous with independence. Educators and psychologists interested in high school students' development define *autonomy* as the students' perception that they can determine their own goals, intentions, and actions regarding learning. Autonomy can also be thought of as the internal state of agency students feel when they perceive that they have control over a situation or outcome (Deci & Ryan, 1985, 1991). This sense of agency, control, and self-determination is a central factor in intrinsic motivation to learn (Ryan & Deci, 2000b). Most teachers would like their students to willingly choose to engage, to learn, and to take control of and responsibility for their actions. This chapter presents information about autonomy and how to support it in the high school science classroom.

WHY IS AUTONOMY IMPORTANT?

An Empirically Supported Theory

Self-determination theory (SDT), one of the most empirically supported and comprehensive models of human motivation, identifies autonomy as one of three basic psychological needs that underlie human behavior (Ryan & Deci, 2000b). Along with the need to feel autonomous, this perspective states that humans also have an innate need to feel both competent and related to others. These two needs are discussed in greater detail in other chapters (see Chapter 6 for a discussion of competence and Chapter 3 for a discussion of relatedness [affiliation]). Basic assumptions of SDT include the idea that people are curious and driven to understand the world around them. Curiosity about their surroundings suggests that students will be interested in science and choose to learn because science offers a way to satisfy their curiosity about natural phenomena. SDT also postulates that intrinsic motivation is maintained over time as a result of having psychological needs satisfied.

A Basic Need

SDT posits that people need to feel autonomous and enjoy being able to make choices and direct their own behavior. Similarly, people dislike feeling that they are being externally controlled and often psychologically resist coercion. In a classroom, students who perceive that they have a sense of control and agency have greater intrinsic motivation toward academic tasks and are less deterred by obstacles, more engaged in learning, and more likely to pursue assignments or learning about a subject area beyond what is required by teachers or tests (Reeve, 2006; Reeve & Jang, 2006).

Autonomy Advances Student Success

Autonomy is also important, because it operates together with other intrinsic motivational processes to bolster students' drive to learn and succeed. In Chapter 6, we discuss the importance of perceived success in fostering students' motivation to learn. A sense of autonomy must be present in order for perceived competence to sustain motivation (Ryan & Deci, 2000b) and is thus an essential ingredient in motivating students to pursue science.

Autonomy Is Fundamental to Adolescent Development

Yet another reason that autonomy is an important concept for a high school science teacher to understand is that autonomy is a central developmental task of adolescence. The physical, cognitive, and social changes of adolescence bring autonomy seeking to the fore as adolescents work to construct their identity, make decisions among a host of alternatives, and cope with increasing responsibilities (Steinberg, 2008). As a result of these developmental factors, autonomy seeking tends to be pronounced among most high school students.

Inquiry Requires Autonomy

Beyond the reasons already mentioned, autonomy is a concept central to the inquiry approach, an important science education method that is both embedded in science education standards (http://www.nextgenscience.org) and endorsed by science teachers' professional organizations (National Science Teachers Association, 2004). The very nature of inquiry requires students to manifest their curiosity and autonomy by asking questions and determining how to answer them.

Teachers Can Make a Difference

Finally, teachers (and other adults) can learn to become autonomy supportive (Reeve, 2006). Because the ability to support autonomy is *not* a fixed trait but a disposition that can be developed, it is important for teachers to learn about it so they can choose whether and how to integrate it with their own practice. Fortunately, evidence suggests that teachers who receive professional development about supporting student autonomy do become more autonomy supportive. Although autonomy is not something that can be given or transmitted directly, teachers can enhance, nurture, and support autonomy in their students. Being autonomy supportive entails embracing an attitude as much or more than implementing a list of techniques.

WHAT HAVE RESEARCHERS DISCOVERED ABOUT AUTONOMY IN SCIENCE CLASSROOMS?

The research findings presented in this section focus on outcomes associated with student reports of how much control and choice they feel they have in high school science classrooms and on teachers' autonomy supporting behaviors. Some of those findings come from our own Science-in-the-Moment (SciMo) Project. General reviews or meta-analysis of educational research also are mentioned when studies on science classes exclusively are not available.

Control and Choice Matter

During the SciMo study, we signaled students at random points during science class to report their thoughts and feelings. Of the more than 4,000 reports we gathered, students told us that they had little or no control in 41 percent of them. They reported having some control in 34 percent of these moments and very much control in only 25 percent of them. Though students did not often feel in control, when they did, many other good things came with that. When students felt that their learning environment was under their control, they also reported higher levels of engagement, higher self-esteem, higher perceived success, and reduced anxiety (Kalkman & DeFrates-Densch, 2011; Schmidt, Kackar, & Strati, 2010; Schmidt, Strati, & Kackar, 2010). These results are consistent with findings from a study conducted in college organic chemistry classes—a subject that many students find difficult. Students who rated their instructor as autonomy supportive reported an increase in perceived success, interest, enjoyment, and self-regulation and a decrease in anxiety over the semester (Black & Deci, 2000).

In our research with the SciMo project, we learned a great deal about how students' sense of autonomy may depend on the activities they do in science class. For example, Kalkman and DeFrates-Densch (2011) found that students felt the most control during student presentations and, not

woodleywonderworks

surprisingly, reported the least control during testing. Students also provided reports of whether they had any choices (yes/no) during ongoing activities. Those reports mirrored, to a considerable extent, their reports of having a sense of control. They reported having the most choices during presentations (followed closely by discussion and lab) and fewest choices during testing (followed closely by lecture). Seatwork, a relatively common activity, was typically (more than half of the time) perceived as affording some choice.

While choice and control are certainly related, they do not always go together. For example, there may be situations where students did not feel that they had any choice in how to do an activity, but they felt great control in executing the externally imposed courses of action. For example, students might have to follow prescribed lab procedures to ensure safety and measurement accuracy, but they can still feel a sense of being in charge of their experiment. Thus in considering autonomy, it is important to consider both choice and control.

Girls Perceive Fewer Choices in Their Science Learning

We have found some gender differences when we look at this fine distinction between choice and control in the SciMo study. While there were no striking gender differences in the general sense of control students felt during activities in science class, female students perceived that they had fewer choices in science activities than their male counterparts. Female students were especially likely to report that they had no choices when they were doing laboratory activities (Schmidt, Kackar et al., 2010).

Autonomy Support Promotes Engagement and Learning

Autonomy support by teachers is linked to engagement and learning; when teachers are more supportive of students' autonomy, students engage more deeply in classroom activities. Strati's analysis of the SciMo data showed that high school science students reported greater cognitive engagement, more success, and less anxiety when their teachers provided more rather than fewer choices (Strati, 2011; Strati & Schmidt, 2012). Other analyses conducted with the SciMo data (Kalkman, DeFrates-Densch, Smith, & Ochoa-Angrino, 2010) linked students' ratings of their teachers' autonomy support with their attitudes toward science. Students who rated their teachers as more autonomy supportive had more positive attitudes toward science, believing that science is interesting, enjoyable, and important.

An early study by Benware and Deci (1984) tested the impact of autonomy support experimentally. The researchers divided college students into two groups. Each group was asked to learn the same science content, but one group was told they were to be tested on the content (*extrinsic control condition*) and one group was told they would be teaching the content to another student (*autonomy supportive condition*). Students in the autonomy-supportive condition learned the content more deeply and had higher intrinsic motivation than students in the extrinsic control condition.

Rewards May Not Work as Well as You Think

A large body of research has established that the use of extrinsic rewards may decrease intrinsic motivation (Deci, Koestner, & Ryan, 1999, 2001). However, teachers are sometimes faced with shepherding students through content and activities that are boring to many of them but nevertheless necessary for progressing in the subject. Many students balk at working hard on such learning tasks. We have observed that most science teachers offer some form of incentive or encouragement to motivate students at such times. Teachers often argue that extrinsic rewards (or punishments) do induce students to perform such tasks and do not seem to undermine intrinsic motivation. Researchers agree that if the task has no intrinsic value for the student, then undermining is not so much the issue. However, they emphasize that a reward still does not do anything to enhance intrinsic motivation (Deci et al., 2001). Further, they explain that extrinsic rewards tend to lead students to simply go through the motions, satisfying minimal teacher requirements, rather than accepting personal responsibility and directing themselves (Ryan & Deci, 2000a). They recommend that teachers who want their students to value and persist in science might want to expend their energy on promoting students' engagement in such tasks by fostering an internal focus using the means suggested in this chapter.

Type of Extrinsic Motivator Impacts Autonomy

Ryan and Deci (2000a) delineated four different types of extrinsic motivation that teachers can and do utilize. They have arranged these types on a continuum from the most externally controlling to the most internally focused. The range represents the difference between a student doing something that is tedious to earn a piece of candy at one end to a student doing the same action because it is something that he or she needs to know to achieve a particular goal. Both students are extrinsically motivated, but the latter is far more autonomous than the former (Ryan & Deci, 2000a). Nicmicc and Ryan (2009) summarized research on the educational outcomes associated with teachers' use of each type of extrinsic motivation. Because each outcome predicts very different student responses, many teachers will want to know about the distinctions between them.

The most controlling and least autonomy-supportive technique is enticing students to perform by using rewards or punishments. This approach is one that we have seen teachers use frequently in classrooms. A substantial body of research indicates that such an externally grounded approach might get students to comply, which has the unfortunate consequence of suggesting to the teacher that the approach is effective, despite the fact that it is unlikely to foster any further learning or investment on the students' part (Niemiec & Ryan, 2009). The second type of external motivation offered by teachers, recognizing or praising students for working or chastising them for not, is considered less controlling than the first. Again, students seem to respond by working. However, students who work for recognition from others or to satisfy their ego will be unlikely to continue their learning in the absence of outside acknowledgement.

The third approach crosses the midline on the control to autonomy support continuum. This approach entails telling the students why it is valuable for them to engage in an activity or learn material that does not appear to be interesting to them. Such an explanation appeals to students, because they feel as if they are deciding to do the work for a good reason. Finally, using the fourth approach, teachers can encourage students to learn content, because it is consistent with a particular identity, interest, goal, or value the students hold. That approach is intrinsically focused and has the highest chance of promoting deeper conceptual understanding and cognitive engagement with the content.

A True Inquiry Approach Is Difficult to Achieve

As mentioned in the section explaining why autonomy is important for high school science teachers, the inquiry approach is consistent with autonomy-supportive environments in that it promotes student control of their learning and enables students to make choices. Unfortunately, we observed two patterns related to inquiry in the classrooms we studied. One pattern was that teachers described their approach as inquiry but did not actually use an inquiry approach. Rather, they provided cookbook-type laboratory experiences that were teacher centered and consequently less likely to promote autonomy than inquiry labs. The other pattern that was prevalent, especially among the less-experienced teachers, was a misinterpretation of *inquiry* as meaning *without guidance* so that students were left to flounder in a chaotic environment and were not provided with constructive feedback or sufficient guidance. Students who are engaged in posing their own questions or designing their own experiments are exercising both choice and control.

Families Influence Students' Autonomy

Numerous studies have shown that parents can either influence or undermine student autonomy development (Chirkov & Ryan, 2001; Grolnick, Ryan, & Deci, 1991; Ratelle, Larose, Guay, & Senecal, 2005; Wong, 2008). Given the substantial impact of parents on adolescents' autonomy development and school success, parents can serve as valued partners in the quest to assist students in developing volitional control of their science education.

Parents often look to teachers for information about homework and studying. Teachers can influence parents to provide autonomy support to their children by offering choices about when to do their homework and some control over how to approach it. Teachers can also communicate with parents about the importance of promoting self-regulation, encourage parents to use types of motivators that support greater autonomy, and provide study resources to help students complete work independently on their class websites that can be accessed from home.

HOW CAN TEACHERS FOSTER AUTONOMY?

As can be seen from the results of classroom studies, teachers can promote student learning and development through autonomy-supportive practices or undermine it by exerting too much control. This section of the chapter provides some practical suggestions for supporting autonomy and encouraging self-control rather than external control. The goal of autonomy support is to "identify, nurture and develop the inner motivational resources that already exist in students" and to boost students' ability to self-regulate (Reeve & Halusic, 2009, p. 146). Our suggestions for autonomy-supportive teaching include the five key ideas presented in Figure 4.1.

Figure 4.1   Suggestions for Autonomy-Supportive Teaching

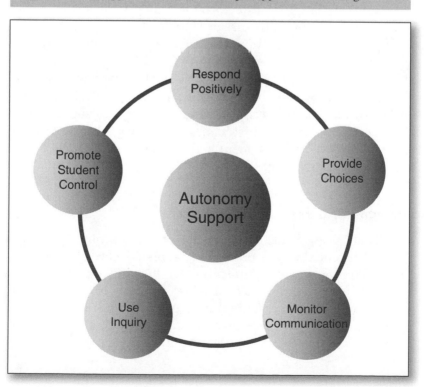

Respond Positively

Autonomy-supportive teachers are student centered; controlling teachers are teacher centered. At the simplest level, student centeredness can be measured by the amount of time teachers spend listening to students, recognizing student contributions, and acknowledging student perspectives (Reeve & Halusic, 2009). Responsiveness to student questions (Reeve & Jang, 2006), especially recognition of and appreciation for authentic questions (those driven by curiosity; e.g., "Why does that happen?" or "How come they did that?"), rewards students' intrinsic curiosity and communicates the importance of students' thinking and interest.

Autonomy-supportive teachers also recognize students' perspectives by accepting negative feelings and allowing the expression of negative feedback (Katz & Assor, 2007). That information can be valuable when modifying lessons to be more engaging or for identifying what students need. Whenever possible, teachers might seek to develop more interesting and enjoyable ways to learn topics that students find boring (Deci et al., 2001). Teachers might also respond to students by saying things like "I know that making those graphs was tedious for you. Did anyone figure out an easier way to make them?" or "I understand that you find dissection upsetting. What might make it easier for you to manage?" Students consequently engage more, because they learn that the teacher cares about their perspectives and will work with them to make the task "worth doing" (Reeve & Halusic, 2009). We do not mean to suggest that teachers should concern themselves with being entertainers of their students. Rather, we believe that there are ways to respond to student boredom and anxiety that will be more or less motivating.

Provide Choices

Emphasizing student ownership of the learning process is another essential way of promoting autonomy development. This can be done by providing students with choices. Teachers can give students meaningful choices in class activities in a number of ways. For example, students can be given options about how to learn particular content. Students can be given the choice of whether to work independently or with a partner. They can be allowed to choose which problem to start working on in a given set of problems. Students also can be offered a variety of learning supports or instructional materials and encouraged to select and use those that help them learn particular content the best. For instance, a variety of alternative texts, Khan Academy tutorials, or other multimedia materials which present and explain the content can be made available, and teachers can encourage students to choose to utilize those materials to complete assignments and to deepen their understanding independently.

Some content studied in science lends itself to independent research, projects, and presentations. Students must make many choices in order to complete a project or presentation in selecting (a) a topic, (b) learning materials, and (c) a mode of presentation. Autonomy is also supported by giving the students responsibility for teaching about their topic. Two of the teachers shown in the companion video clips on our website provide their students with the option of planning and conducting field trips for elementary and middle school students through the school's woods.

Monitor Communication

Students tend to be sensitive to the tone of communication from teachers, so it behooves teachers who aspire to an autonomy-supportive style to monitor their communication patterns with students (Katz & Assor, 2007). Choices offered in a directive manner are not perceived by most students as true options. Teachers might consider how often they use controlling words (*should, must, have to*) and how often they use invitational language (*could, might, suggest,* and *what do you think?*). Teachers also will get insight by monitoring how their students use these words when referring to their class work.

Emphasizing students' cognitive agency is of primary importance in science classrooms. Controlling teachers tend to criticize students by saying things such as "You need to work harder if you want to learn to balance these chemical equations," or by giving students a directive, such as "First do *x*, then do *y*." Autonomy-supportive teachers say things such as "I notice you are struggling with balancing these chemical equations. What are you finding difficult about it?" and then leading the student to figure out a strategy that makes sense to them. Students who are provided with informational feedback and scaffolding learn to take responsibility for and to solve their own problems (Black & Deci, 2000), an optimal outcome from the point of view of both teachers and students. Teachers will want to be careful not to offer students help if they do not need it, because that is especially undermining of student autonomy (Katz & Assor, 2007). In our observations, this tended to happen more frequently with female than male students. We recommend that teachers observe briefly before intervening to be sure that the student really is struggling and work to socialize students to ask for help when they need it.

Use an Inquiry Approach

The use of inquiry methodology in science fits well with an emphasis on cognitive agency. Practices that support inquiry and autonomy include (1) a central focus on student interests, curiosity, and perspective; (2) structuring the environment to support active discovery and interaction with materials rather than teacher-centered demonstrations; (3) guiding students to reason through a problem, providing hints or reminders that require them to make connections rather than telling them the answer or providing a worked-through model before they have tried to figure it out; and (4) engaging students in conversations about the interpretation of data.

A word about classroom structure is important here. According to Reeve and Halusic (2009), teachers often equate structure with control, yet autonomy-supportive teachers actually tend to provide greater structure than controlling teachers. Designing assignments, classrooms, and laboratories to support student choice, inquiry, and independent work is challenging, but the ground work in advance pays off in helping students develop their inner resources. Autonomy-supportive structures include setting clear expectations, identifying an array of resources, and arranging physical space to promote interaction with materials and peer collaboration as well as establishing routines for providing constructive feedback in writing or through scheduled opportunities.

Teachers' explanation of why it is important to understand a particular concept or how it is related to their interests or things they consider important supports student autonomy. A rationale provides students with a reason to choose to learn or to participate and supports internalization and self-direction. In Chapter 2, we elaborated on the importance of connecting the content being studied in science class with the practical applications of the material. The interested reader can refer to that chapter to learn more. Rationales that take adolescent students' perspectives into account also can be useful. Teachers might say things such as, "I know the safety goggles are not stylish, but without them, your eyes could be injured" (Reeve, 2006).

Promote Student Control

Another way to support autonomy is to actively resist the pressure to depend upon external controls such as rewards, punishments, and micro management. Teachers have been placed under enormous pressure since the advent of high-stakes testing and the evaluation of teachers based on those tests (Ryan & Brown, 2005), and there is a natural inclination to get results as quickly as possible. In order to expedite the learning process, many teachers resort to trying to exert control over their students. It may seem counterintuitive, but controlling classroom practices (as described above) set up a vicious cycle whereby exerting external control saps students' enjoyment and agency, students disengage, and teachers need to exert even greater external control to obtain student compliance with lessons (Niemiec & Ryan, 2009).

Parents Can Be Valuable Allies in Promoting Student Autonomy

Parents can serve as an audience or sounding board for student-generated reports, or students can be given the responsibility of teaching material to their parents and discussing lifestyle decisions related to that material. For example, one teacher we observed had students evaluate their families' genetic risk for cancer and their exposure to carcinogens related to their lifestyle choices. Students then taught their families about how to avoid exposure to carcinogens and how to use screening to monitor their health. Teachers also can provide suggestions to parents for how to support their students' homework completion in autonomy-supportive and less-controlling ways. See the companion website for examples of how this might be done.

WHAT RESOURCES ARE AVAILABLE TO SCIENCE TEACHERS FOR PROMOTING STUDENT AUTONOMY?

The companion website, http://www.niu.edu/eteams, contains resources that can aid teachers in promoting student autonomy in their classrooms or that can be recommended for parents of their students. The following and more can be found on the website:

- Links to tutorials that students can choose to help themselves understand content and complete assignments
- Links to articles and background materials on supporting autonomy in the classroom
- Streaming video clips of science teachers using autonomy-supportive practices and a scientist remembering autonomy supportive practices in high school classrooms
- Additional readings on using the inquiry method

CHAPTER FIVE

Confidence

Joe Lorenzo, a physical science teacher, is scoring his students' exams. As he writes a "C" on Luisa's, he is filled with regret and frustration. "She knows this stuff, but her answers are vague," he says to himself. "I can see when she talks with her classmates that she understands this, but all of her comments start with 'I don't really know, but...' or 'I don't think this is right, but...' If she just had confidence, she would do so much better. What can I do to convince her that she can do this?"

Most teachers and parents don't need to see a lot of research to be convinced that confidence contributes to success. One of us (Jennifer) recalls being told repeatedly by a high school coach that "you have to believe it to achieve it." In this chapter, we will only briefly review the research, which confirms what most teachers and parents already know about the importance of confidence. We will focus more on where confidence comes from and how the factors that shape students' confidence for science may be different for boys and girls. We will then offer practical suggestions for teachers who want to help students improve their confidence.

WHAT DOES IT MEAN TO HAVE CONFIDENCE IN SCIENTIFIC ABILITIES?

Confidence is an everyday term describing the beliefs people hold about their potential to achieve an outcome. We decided to use this term precisely because it is familiar to teachers and parents. Our use of the term is compatible with, and informed by, terms such as *self-efficacy* (Bandura, 1986) and *expectancies for success* (Eccles et al., 1983; Wigfield & Eccles, 2000, 2002), which are used by educational psychologists. These less-commonly used educational psychology terms refer to beliefs about succeeding (a) in particular domains, such as physics, biology, writing, or basketball, and (b) on specific tasks, such as using a pipette or memorizing the noble gases.

WHY IS CONFIDENCE IMPORTANT?

Students' confidence contributes to what they choose to do and how they approach that choice. When a student has confidence, he or she tends to engage in activities more readily, work harder, and continue trying longer (Schunk & Miller, 2002). It should come as no surprise, then, that students tend to learn and achieve more as a result of higher confidence levels.

The high school years are a critically important time for the development of confidence. Confidence comes into sharp relief during adolescence, because the many developmental and environmental changes experienced by adolescents present challenges that require them to adapt and adjust. As students accommodate to those changes, they go through a self-appraisal process that includes comparing themselves to others and to standards that have generally become more demanding. This can take a toll on students' sense of confidence under the best of circumstances, so their confidence frequently declines across typical adolescent transition points, such as the move from elementary school to middle school and then from middle school to high school (Schunk & Miller, 2002; Wigfield & Tonks, 2002).

Although there is considerable variation within gender, an overall gender gap in confidence regarding science and science-related activities appears during high school, with girls losing far

more confidence than boys (Andre, Whigham, Hendrickson, & Chambers, 1999; Greenfield, 1996). We investigated high school students' confidence in science over the course of a single school year and found that not only did girls begin the year with less confidence than boys, but they were also more likely than boys to decline in confidence over the course of the year. Importantly, the extent and pattern of that change varied considerably between teachers, suggesting that teachers have the power to fend off a decline in confidence among their female students (Schmidt & Shumow, 2012). Indeed, classroom environments are very important for influenc-
ing confidence (Lloyd, Walsh, & Yailagh, 2005). Teachers can and do impact students' confidence in science and can be more effective if they know the information and have access to the resources presented in this chapter.

RDaniel Shutterstock

WHAT HAVE RESEARCHERS DISCOVERED ABOUT CONFIDENCE?

Confidence Comes From Many Sources

It is important for teachers to know what contributes to students' confidence in a way that promotes achievement motivation. Bandura (1986, 1997) specifies four major sources of confidence. These sources can promote or undermine students' confidence. Of course, students' background characteristics may result in differing degrees of access to these important influences.

Prior Success

The first source of confidence is a history of prior success (also called *mastery experiences*). Researchers from a number of different theoretical traditions have identified prior success (or failure) as a primary contributor to a student's confidence (Bandura, 1986, 1997; Eccles, 1983; Wigfield & Eccles, 2000, 2002). A person's history of prior success refers to the degree to which he or she has experienced success in a given domain, such as science. This is reflected in performance on particular tasks such as test taking, laboratory experiences, or writing laboratory reports. Chapter 6 addresses the role of success in depth.

Observing Others

The second influence on confidence is observing the experience of others (also referred to as *vicarious experience*). Students learn from a wide variety of role models and, if a role model is perceived as similar to oneself, the influence is strengthened (Schunk & Hanson, 1985). For example, models close to an adolescent's age tend to have a greater effect than do adult models. However, adult role models can be influential, and in these cases, the same principle of similarity applies. A ninth-grade Spanish-speaking girl who was born in Mexico and is now living in Southern California is unlikely to see Stephen Hawking's success as a physicist as an indicator that she, too, could be a physicist. Exposure to an older woman from her neighborhood who emigrated from Latin America, obtained a college degree in physics, and works at NASA's Jet Propulsion Laboratory would likely have a far greater impact on her sense of what she herself can attain. Similarly, parents can serve as role models through careers and interests. Teachers should note that observing others struggle, cope, and eventually succeed at a task can contribute to confidence even more than watching someone for whom the task appears to come very easily. Conversely, watching a peer fail, especially one with whom the student identifies, can lead a student to expect failure.

Persuasion

Persuasion, the third influence on confidence, entails efforts to convince students that they can be successful and to urge them to try a particular task. Persuasion often takes the form of verbal encouragement, such as "I'm sure you can do it." Encouragement can be most effective if the task is within the student's reach, but it can also be damaging if the task is out of reach and the student fails miserably. Students' confidence in themselves and in the teacher (or coach or parent) can be undermined when adult persuasion is based on unrealistic expectations, whether too high or too low. An example of expectations being too low often occurs when stereotypes lead adults to think that certain students cannot or will not do well. Constructive feedback on student assignments can also operate as a form of persuasion when it is given in a way that tells students what they did that enabled them to be successful or convinces students that they are capable of improving by following specific suggestions (Schunk & Miller, 2002).

Emotional Experiences

The final source of confidence is how students feel when they are in class or working on a particular task (also referred to as *physiological responses*). Feeling stressed or anxious in class undermines confidence. On the other hand, feeling good emotionally (enjoying oneself, feeling interested) while engaged in a learning situation is likely to promote self-confidence (Stipek, 1998). The impact of emotional experience is explored in depth in Chapter 10.

The Sources of Confidence in Science May Be Different for Boys and Girls

In our research, we have found that these sources of confidence in science may operate slightly differently for boys than for girls, with some sources exerting greater influence than others. It is important to note that these gendered patterns in the sources of science confidence do not operate the same way in subject areas such as English (Pajares, Johnson, & Usher, 2007). In other words, boys and girls appear to develop their confidence for science in unique ways.

Mastery Experiences Influence Boys More Than Girls

We found that girls' prior success experiences did not seem to have the positive effect on confidence that theory and prior research have suggested. Among girls in our study, the students with higher science grades did not have higher science confidence than their less successful peers. Thus objective successes did not have a positive influence on confidence. As a matter of fact, we found that girls generally reported feeling less successful than boys in science, even when their grades were higher. So focusing only on creating opportunities for girls to achieve objective success may not be the most effective route to increasing girls' confidence in science. It may be most effective to couple supporting successful science achievement with other factors as described below. These types of objective success experiences, however, do appear to be the most highly motivating experiences among male students (Lent, Lopez, Brown, & Gore, 1996).

Persuasion and Observing Others Are Effective Strategies for Influencing Girls' Confidence in Their Scientific Abilities

A number of researchers have found that persuasion and vicarious experiences are particularly influential sources of motivation for girls in mathematics, life science, and physical science (Britner, 2008; Lent, Brown, Gover, & Nijjer, 1996; Zeldin & Pajares, 2000). Role models show female students that science is an attainable and approachable field (Society of Women Engineers-Assessing Women and Men in Engineering Project [SWE-AWE], 2009), and successful female scientists often point to role models as having been highly motivating to them (Zeldin & Pajares, 2000). In a study of women who had attained success in science, technology, engineering, and mathematics (STEM) fields, Zeldin and Pajares (2000) reported that many women identified supportive and encouraging high school teachers as instrumental to their success. In our research, student ratings of their science teachers' confidence in them (which we interpreted as a form of persuasion) predicted students' own confidence, though it was not related to change in confidence over time.

Emotional Experience Matters for Girls

Emotional experience in science also appears to exert particularly strong influence on girls' confidence in their abilities. In our research, girls were far more likely than boys to report feeling stressed in science, and feeling stressed during class was related to a decline in their confidence. Britner (2008) also found that negative emotional states such as anxiety and stress play a prominent role in lowering female students' self-confidence in science, but these same emotions do not exert such strong influence on males' science confidence.

Teachers Are an Important
Source of Science Confidence

In several studies, female students have attributed their confidence about doing well in STEM fields to their teachers' qualities more often than have male students (Britner, 2008; Lent, Brown et al., 1996). Given girls' attributions and the different patterns of change in student confidence that we observed in different teachers' classrooms in our study, we set out to learn more about how teachers' practices were related to changes in boys' and girls' confidence (Schmidt & Shumow, 2012). To do so, we looked carefully at the practices of three female biology teachers. In one teacher's class, both male and female students increased in confidence over the school year. In another teacher's class, boys' and girls' confidence levels remained static. Boys' confidence levels in the remaining teacher's class increased but girls decreased in confidence. These findings tied teacher practices to student perceptions.

When we analyzed each teacher's interaction patterns with students, we saw that the ways teachers interacted with students was consistent with changes in students' self-efficacy in their classroom. The teacher whose students grew more confident engaged her students and promoted their thinking far more than did the teacher whose students did not change. We interpreted the way she called on and interacted with her students as a form of persuasion to participate in learning. Furthermore, this teacher engaged her male and female students at equal rates. The teacher whose male students improved but whose female students declined engaged her male students nearly twice as often as her female students. The teacher whose students did not change did little to encourage her students to participate. In our interviews with the teachers, we ascertained that the teachers' beliefs about gender differences and equity in science aligned with their practices and with their students' confidence.

The fact that female students' confidence is often low initially, drops across the school year, and is related to the teacher's beliefs and practices highlights the importance of trying to intervene. Girls' confidence in science, rather than objective measures of achievement, appears to be the central factor in whether or not they continue to study or choose careers in science (i.e., their motivation for studying science). It is important to remember that one of the teachers we studied reversed the general trend through her efforts. Teachers may want to try some of the suggestions and use some of the resources provided in the following sections, so as not to contribute to a loss of confidence in their students.

Families Influence Confidence

Parents exert a powerful impact on their children's confidence (Frome & Eccles, 1998). We found that parental involvement at school predicted students' in-the-moment confidence when they were engaged in science classroom activities (Shumow, Lyutykh, & Schmidt, 2011) but did not contribute to change in their general science confidence during the school year (Schmidt & Shumow, 2012). In other words, parents influenced their children's daily motivation and engagement. Parental involvement at school (e.g., attending events, volunteering, talking to teachers) might serve to communicate to students that school is important. Other researchers have highlighted the role of parents as role models themselves, as providers of role models (e.g., finding, recognizing, and pointing out female scientists in person or in the media), and as cheerleaders who encourage their children's efforts and success in science (SWE-AWE, 2009).

HOW CAN TEACHERS BUILD STUDENT CONFIDENCE?

There are at least four approaches that can be used to build confidence. Those are described here.

Promote Success

As noted earlier in this chapter, successful experiences play an important role in predicting students' levels of confidence. It is important to remember that for female students, the role of success may be strengthened by pairing it with images of role models and providing encouragement. The role of success and how to promote it is so central in motivating students to learn science and in the work of a science teacher that we have devoted an entire chapter to it (see Chapter 6).

Make Use of Role Models

Science teachers can arrange a variety of role models for their students, making sure that those models include females and racial or ethnic minorities. We have seen science teachers use students in their classrooms as effective role models from time to time by having a student show a particularly effective strategy or approach that they were using to complete a lab or other assignment. Notice that the focus is on a specific strategy or process that peers can use and not on some fixed ability (see Chapter 8). Choosing a specific instance opens the door to being able to highlight the success of a number of different students over time rather than just a few. The experienced high school teacher knows that peers influence one another, and given the research evidence that peer models are the most influential, this technique is especially promising.

Students can be asked to identify family, friends, or community members who might serve as role models, but role models do not have to be people whom the students know or with whom they interact directly. In other words, these role models can be presented using various media. Recall that students benefit most when they see models similar to themselves, so it is important to present models with different characteristics to increase the chance that all students will find an effective model (male/female, race/ethnicity, people with disabilities). Teachers can invite former students who have entered science careers to come back and talk to students. A highly acclaimed chemistry professor we know searches his undergraduate classes for female students who do well and who look like they are affiliated with different peer crowds (e.g., preppie, alternative) and from underrepresented groups; he then recruits them to do demonstrations in middle schools and high schools so that the adolescents see that people similar to them succeed in science.

An important caveat for teachers to consider in their identification of role models, however, is that when learners are anxious about their abilities to begin with, they tend to be intimidated by role models who look as though they never struggled and, instead, will learn more from role models who used to struggle with the material but, through their efforts, were able to achieve the competence that they demonstrate today. For struggling learners, seeing that someone else struggled and eventually succeeded can be highly motivating. This may be true especially for girls in science, who tend to have greater levels of anxiety than boys.

Encourage Students, Especially Girls

Encouragement (i.e., persuasion) contributes to student confidence. There is some evidence demonstrating that when teachers simply tell students that they believe that they can do something, this alone improves confidence. Encouragement is especially important for female students. It is important to remember that person praise ("You are so smart") is different from encouragement ("If you continue to use the study strategies you used this year, I am sure you'll be successful in AP physics next year"). Science teachers, guidance counselors, and parents can encourage girls to take higher-level science courses. If female students hear the message that they are equally capable of achieving in science, then they are more likely to assess their abilities more accurately (Hill, Corbett, & St. Rose, 2010). Encourage students to think about careers that they might not have considered and persuade them that they are good candidates for these science-based careers if such persuasion is warranted.

Communicate With Families

Science teachers can let families know about how influential they can be in building students' confidence through an announcement made at an open house or in an electronic or print communication. Parents can also benefit from understanding the potential differences between boys and girls when trying to encourage their children. Family members might have suggestions for potential role models. They might also appreciate written information and links to role models, posted on a class website. Families can provide more encouragement if they are aware of the career opportunities afforded by studying science and if they are encouraged to model interest in their children's science class and to talk about and explore careers in science with their children. Keep parents informed of local science activities and events they can share with their child and invite them to contact you if they need more information or support for their child's science study.

WHAT RESOURCES CAN SCIENCE TEACHERS USE TO PROMOTE CONFIDENCE?

The companion website, http://www.niu.edu/eteams, contains useful resources to help teachers build confidence in their students or to recommend for parents of their students. The following and more can be found on the website:

- Links to sources that provide examples of women as science role models
- Links to professional organizations where classroom resources and guest speakers may be found
- Links for resources to help students with test-taking anxiety
- Streaming video clips of women role models in science and teachers who positively impact their students' confidence and competence
- Links and videos of interest to parents

CHAPTER SIX

Success

| *Michelle sighs as she looks at her chemistry quiz, muttering to herself,*
| *"95! What's wrong with me? I'll never get into medical school if I suck*
| *at chem." Meanwhile, her classmate Alan glances at the 86 scrawled*
| *in red pen at the top of his quiz and high-fives his neighbor Tyler, saying,*
| *"Woo-hoo, I'm a master at this!"*

WHAT IS THE MOTIVATIONAL CONCEPT OF SUCCESS?

This chapter focuses on the role that success plays in fostering students' motivation in science. As such, the chapter discusses the related concepts of mastery experiences (Bandura, 1986), goal setting (not to be confused with goal orientation; see Chapter 7), perceived success (Eccles, 1983), competence (Ryan & Deci, 2000a), and attributions for success or failure (Weiner, 1986, 1992). Although researchers draw upon different theoretical traditions and distinguish among these ideas, the classroom teacher probably will find these concepts highly related in terms of understanding and boosting student motivation to learn in high school science classrooms.

Success in a science classroom can be understood as accomplishing the goals students have set for themselves or others have set for them. That definition calls attention to the importance of goal setting. High school students' goals (or those that their teachers and parents hold for them) can be long-term goals, such as graduating from high school; being admitted to the college of their choice; or becoming a doctor, physicist, or food scientist. Goals can also be short term, such as finishing a lab report, doing well on a quiz, or completing a scholarship application. Typically, students who experience the most success are able to break goals into subgoals (Locke & Latham, 2002; Schunk, 2011). These students also have high expectations for their own achievement and are adept at setting achievable goals. Adult guidance is initially needed to help students get to the point of setting achievable subgoals independently.

Self-determination theory (SDT) identifies competence as an inherent need that drives individuals to seek out and manage situations in which they can experience success and perceive themselves as successful individuals (Deci & Ryan, 1985, 1991; see also Chapters 3 [Affiliation] and 4 [Autonomy] for the other needs identified by SDT). It is important to recognize that perceiving oneself as successful or competent is not always the same as having attained external markers of success such as points, good grades, high test scores, or admission to a college of choice. Michelle, for example, does not feel successful on her quiz, although most observers would think that she had succeeded and she has, indeed, met an objective marker of success.

Another term that is important to understanding the motivational concept of success is *attribution*. Attributions refer to reasons

people use to explain success or failure to themselves or others (Weiner, 1992). These reasons can be characterized as either *internal* (about the individual) or *external* (about the situation), as changeable or stable, and as controllable or uncontrollable. From a motivational perspective, the reasons that students use to explain their

Photo by Steve Stern

academic successes and failures are as important or perhaps more important than whether the student failed or succeeded, as you will see in the sections that follow.

WHY IS SUCCESS AN IMPORTANT MOTIVATIONAL CONCEPT?

Success Builds Confidence and Pride

The old adage "nothing succeeds like success" is apt. Success is motivating: We are more likely to pursue a task if we have had past success with it and feel competent doing it (Eccles, 1983). Success builds confidence and pride. Researchers have shown repeatedly that perceiving the self as competent is a precursor to long-term success. Students' beliefs about whether they are competent and successful can profoundly affect their activity choices, persistence, and effort (Pajares, n.d.). As seen in the chapter on confidence (Chapter 5), it is also important to believe that success is within reach—the motivational concepts of confidence and success are intertwined.

How Adults Explain Success Matters

The attributions (or reasons) a person has for success or failure on a given task predict how much they will engage in similar tasks and try to succeed in the future. Specifically, students are more likely to keep trying if they believe that they have control over the outcome, and they will expect to succeed if they think that their ability and/or the situation are amenable to change (Weiner, 1986, 1992). If teachers and mentors understand the conditions under which students' beliefs about success and failure work to promote or undermine learning, they can use that knowledge to further their aims to help students succeed.

Promoting Students' Success Is Fundamental to Teaching

How teachers structure the learning environment and the feedback they provide to their students will have a profound impact on students' mastery experiences, perceptions of success, and motivation to learn. Clear explanations, constructive feedback, and goal setting contribute to student success. The way students and teachers explain successes (and failures) also impacts students' ability beliefs and future effort. Students internalize what their teachers and parents say about why they have succeeded or failed, which influences students' own attributions about learning.

Most high school students *do* benefit from having their teachers inspire them to develop and set both short- and long-term goals. Helping them through the short-term obstacles can be very important. Of course, there are individual differences among students—some students need more support and encouragement than others. In fact, some, similar to Michelle in this chapter's opening vignette, need a great deal of support, even though they are students teachers are likely to think of as quite successful.

WHAT HAVE RESEARCHERS DISCOVERED ABOUT SUCCESS IN SCIENCE CLASSROOMS?

Students Need the Right Kind of Praise to Be Motivated

Some researchers have found that perceiving oneself as successful is equivalent to being confident about being successful in the future (Eccles, 1983). Not surprisingly, students who receive positive process feedback (feedback that focuses on what they did to achieve a good outcome rather than simply acknowledging the good outcome) are more likely to perceive themselves as successful. On the other hand, students who are told their work is poor are likely to perceive themselves as unsuccessful and, consequently, to be less motivated to pursue learning (Ryan & Deci, 2000b). Of course, if the work is too easy for them and they recognize praise as false, most students will not develop a sense of competence or motivation to succeed. Quite the contrary: Excessive praise for easily accomplished tasks can undermine motivation by giving students the implicit message that their teacher does not see them as capable. Teachers need to balance the complexities of providing students with challenging tasks, giving them appropriate tools for succeeding at those tasks, and establishing real potential for success in order to promote optimal motivation (Miller, 1998).

How You Explain Success and Failure Is Important

The extent to which students attribute their successes or failures to controllable, internal, and changeable factors plays a role in whether they think they are competent or not (Weiner, 1992). People tend to attribute their successes and failures to their ability, to the amount or type of effort they put into the task, to characteristics of the task at hand, to others (a teacher, peers), and sometimes even to luck. Possible attributions to luck mean that the outcome was random, external, and uncontrollable, so there is no reason to invest in learning or effort. Attributions to ability are internal and often (in the U.S.) perceived as uncontrollable and unchangeable and, unless the student has a growth mindset (see Chapter 8), will not result in concerted effort. Attributions to others are external, uncontrollable, and unchangeable unless the student sought help proactively. How students perceive the task depends upon characteristics of the task. Most teachers and psychologists hope that students attribute their success to their effort or the strategy they used, because those factors are internal, controllable, and changeable for every student.

Girls Underestimate Their Success in Science

In our study, we found something that researchers (e.g., Carlone, 2004) have been observing in other samples: Girls were as or more successful than boys in their science classes in terms of grades and achievement test scores, but they did not feel that way. Students' in-the-moment reports during the Science-in-the-Moment (SciMo) study revealed that female students felt less successful, less skilled, and less in control than males (Schmidt, Strati, & Kackar, 2010). Importantly, momentary success and control were linked for both male and female students (see Chapter 4 for more about students' perceptions of control).

Female students tend to overestimate the level of scientific and mathematical achievement required to be a science, technology, engineering, or mathematics (STEM) professional. In other words, they do not see themselves as successful enough to be scientists. While it is true that STEM majors need solid achievement and strong skills in science, many female students with achievement records equal to male science and engineering students think they are incapable of succeeding in STEM majors or careers (Hill, Corbett, & St. Rose, 2010). This phenomenon hits close to home. Lee's daughter had established an excellent record in science, and consequently, she was urged by her professors to pursue a doctorate in science. In pursuing a master's degree, she took a class from a female professor who had won the Nobel Prize in a related science.

Lee's daughter subsequently explained that she would not enter the doctoral program, because she did not have and could not imagine ever having her professor's level of knowledge, skill, and "brilliance," which, in her estimation, was what it took to be a real scientist. Several of her male classmates had no such reservations and did not even think to compare themselves to Nobel Prize winners as a standard. This scenario highlights the importance of having highly successful role models highlight their own struggles with the material so that students who may feel a little anxious about their own ability to learn the material feel they can relate to them (for a fuller discussion of this topic, the reader is referred to Chapter 5).

Parents Promote Success

Parents can be powerful allies in promoting student success (Ames, Khoju, & Watkins, 1993; Steinberg, Lamborn, Dornbusch, & Darling, 1992). In our research, we found that when parents were more involved at home in terms of setting expectations for doing science homework, monitoring science homework, finding someone to help students with homework when needed, and setting rules on school nights, their children felt more competent during science classes and devoted more effort to science homework (Shumow, Lyutykh, & Schmidt, 2011). We also found that when students were experiencing real difficulty, parents of high school students did not respond with increased involvement, as they tend to do when their children are younger (Shumow et al., 2011; Shumow & Miller, 2001). It might be helpful for teachers to know that research shows that inviting parents to be involved is a more powerful predictor of parental involvement than other factors, such as socioeconomic status (Simon, 2001).

HOW CAN TEACHERS PROMOTE STUDENT SUCCESS AND ENCOURAGE MOTIVATING ATTRIBUTIONS?

Teachers can do much to promote student success. Several other chapters provide suggestions that are helpful in promoting success; see, for example, the practices recommended in Chapter 4 (Autonomy) and the strategies recommended in Chapter 7 (Goal Orientation). Figure 6.1 summarizes a number of suggestions for teachers.

Figure 6.1 Suggestions for Promoting Student Success

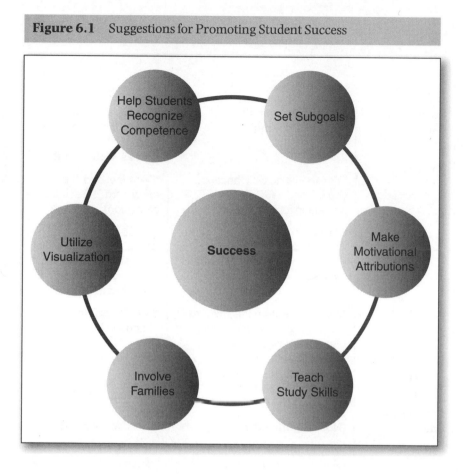

Make Motivational Attributions

Because attributions by teachers (and other adults) impact students, it is important for students to hear the message that both successes and failures are changeable and under the students' control so that students expend effort to learn (Weiner, 1986). We often hear ourselves and the teachers we work with wishing students "good luck" on a test. Of course, we all mean well, but attributions to luck are the most demotivating of all, because they are not changeable or under the student's control, so we have tried to break ourselves of this habit and recommend that other teachers do, too. In Figure 6.2, we present several examples of the types of attributional statements that teachers can make, highlighting those that are most motivating.

Figure 6.2   How Different Teacher Attribution Statements Impact Student Motivation

	Internal Causes	*External Causes*
Controllable Causes	**Effort and Strategies (Most Motivating)**	**Situational Factors: Task Difficulty or Other People (Not as Motivating)**
	"You should do well, because you studied hard." (effort attribution for success)	"Don't feel bad, the test was really hard." (task difficulty attribution)
	"This was a disappointing score; if you study for the next test, you will do better." (effort attribution for failure)	"Those of you who had Mrs. X for algebra can do this; the rest of you cannot." (other attribution for success and failure)
	"If the concepts in this unit are challenging, try approaching them by focusing on each subsection at a time, building on each as you go." (strategy attribution for struggle)	"I'll help you." (other attribution for struggle)
Uncontrollable Causes	**Ability (Not as Motivating)**	**Luck (Least Motivating)**
	"Way to go, you're a regular genius at this!"	"You have the entire class period to work on the test. Good luck!"
	"Maybe you should think about taking the regular section instead of honors; you just don't seem to be a math person."	"It's your lucky day; you got a perfect score on the quiz!"

As a reflection activity, we suggest that you try to rephrase the statements in Figure 6.2 that make attributions to external and/or uncontrollable causes. Rephrase these statements so that they transfer responsibility to student effort and strategy use, which are more motivational attributions. Then, you may refer to the success chapter section of the companion website for examples of how we recommend restating them.

Encourage Students to Set Subgoals

An effective strategy to encourage success is to provide students with guidance and practice in breaking broad learning goals into subgoals. The most effective subgoals are those that are (1) focused on a specific thing (e.g., velocity), (2) quickly attainable (within a day to a week), (3) actions within the student's control (e.g., "Calculate and check the average velocity practice set") rather than an outcome not necessarily within the student's control (e.g., "Get an A"), and (4) able to be determined as complete (Bandura, 1997; Schunk, 2011). Some teachers have found posting daily goals (or learning targets) or lesson objectives on the front board to be highly effective practice.

Provide Access to Extra Help

Many teachers provide extra help to students who are struggling. It can also be beneficial to plan for additional helpers. Tutors can be recruited for students who need skill development. These tutors might be advanced students in the area you teach who will help other students as a service project. Students can also be assigned to a "study buddy" in the class, with the expectation that they will help each other if one student is absent or has a question.

Utilize Visualization

Success in science (and mathematics) oftentimes depends on spatial skills. A number of concepts are more easily grasped visually and understood through spatial reasoning. Science textbooks and reading typically contain graphs, diagrams, and figures. Yet students vary considerably in their spatial skills, which are developed to a considerable extent through experience and practice (Sorby, 2009). Therefore, the more teachers utilize three-dimensional models, allow students to manipulate the models, and have students draw or create their own spatial models, the better. Teachers can also model how to interpret graphs, diagrams, and figures. Female students tend to have less experience and therefore less developed spatial skills than male students, but this need not be destiny. Technology and the Internet are excellent resources to help students with understanding of concepts through the use of both visual and interactive models. Female engineering students who receive spatial visualization training improve considerably and graduate in engineering more frequently than their female classmates who do not receive the training (Sorby & Baartmans, 2000; see Hill et al., 2010 for a review).

Help Female Students Recognize Their Competence

It is important to remember that male and female students may differ in how they assess their competence and develop confidence (Schunk, Pintrich, & Meece, 2008). As we have seen, female students rate their competence and confidence as (a) lower than males, (b) lower than objective measures of their performance, and (c) below required standards for STEM majors, even when objectively qualified. To combat these tendencies, educators can make performance standards and expectations clear to the students (Hill et al., 2010). Teachers can tell students things such as, "If you earned a score of 80 or above, you can conclude that you are doing great. If you did not, then you need to change your study habits or seek help," or teachers can interpret standardized test scores for the students, saying something such as, "You know, this is within the score range of students admitted to college programs in (insert appropriate STEM major); maybe you could think about a career in that field."

Welcome Family Involvement

As seen above, families have an impact on students' success and perceptions of success. Welcome family involvement by providing information they can use to guide their students' goal setting and homework. Invite parents to see students' projects or presentations at school. This requires a small amount of effort in comparison to the potential payoff. Share information with parents about local and regional opportunities such as seminars, camps, museums, programming, and special events that promote involvement in science.

WHAT RESOURCES CAN SCIENCE TEACHERS USE TO PROMOTE SUCCESS?

The companion website, http://www.niu.edu/eteams, contains practical resources to help teachers promote success in their classroom or that can be recommended for parents of their students. The following and more can be found on the website:

- Examples of handouts for students to use to help them set self-goals and subgoals
- Links to articles on goal setting for teens
- Visualization resources
- Examples of charts and other tools to help students monitor their progress
- Streaming video clips of the strategies discussed in this chapter
- Links to parent newsletters that help parents guide their children in setting goals for success

CHAPTER SEVEN

Goal Orientation

Amy is interested in learning as much as she can in biology. Throughout the year, she goes to great lengths to make sure she truly understands the material—asking thoughtful questions in class, revising homework that she had done incorrectly, and asking for feedback. Her commitment to understanding usually results in good grades, but grades are not her main focus. In fact, sometimes she will expend more effort on an assignment with little payoff for a grade. Kristen, on the other hand, has one of the highest grades in her class, and her position at the top of the class is clearly important her. She has a great deal of interest in how her classmates perform on tests and obviously receives pleasure from outperforming her peers. When material is being presented in class, Kristen is often one of the first to ask, "Will this be on the test?" Both Amy and Kristen are highly engaged in achievement behaviors such as preparing for tests, completing homework, and participating in class. The difference between them is their purpose or reasons for engaging in these behaviors. Most of us have had students similar to these in our classes. These two student profiles represent two different achievement goal orientations.

WHAT IS GOAL ORIENTATION?

Goal orientation is a term used by motivation researchers to refer to the overarching purpose or reasons for which a student engages in achievement behaviors (Pintrich, 2003). Rather than referring to a specific goal, such as getting an A on a test, goal orientation represents a complex pattern of beliefs that leads to "different ways of approaching, engaging in, and responding to achievement situations" (Ames, 1992, p. 261). Like Amy, students who approach learning with a *mastery goal orientation* (also called *learning-focused orientation* or *task-focused orientation*) aim to learn as much as possible, to improve their knowledge and skills, and to develop their competence and/or understanding. Students, like Kristen, who have a *performance goal orientation* (also called *ability-focused orientation* or *ego-focused orientation*) are focused on how capable they appear to be in relation to others (Ames, 1992; Dweck & Leggett, 1988; Elliott & Dweck, 1988). This second type of goal orientation can be demonstrated in two different types of student behavior patterns—the *performance approach goal orientation* and the *performance avoidance goal orientation* (Elliot, 1997; VandeWalle, 1997). The performance approach goal orientation is characterized by students wanting to perform better than others or to appear smarter than others—similar to Kristen in the example above—whereas the performance avoidance goal orientation is characterized by students wanting to avoid looking dumb or being judged as less competent than others. Students with a performance approach goal orientation tend to lose interest in a task if they do not have the opportunity to achieve recognition or reward for doing it. Students with a performance avoidance goal orientation will attempt to sidestep or refuse to try tasks at which they think they will fail.

Recent research shows that one's goal orientation is not a stable trait but can vary from situation to situation. People often hold different learning goals for different tasks and can even be motivated by multiple goals for any particular task (Turner, Meyer, Midgley, & Patrick, 2003). Students' goal orientations are malleable and depend, to a considerable extent, on the kinds of educational contexts they experience, particularly the feedback that they receive from adults (Ames, 1992). Those influences are described later in this chapter.

WHY IS GOAL ORIENTATION IMPORTANT?

Students With Mastery Goals Become More Deeply Engaged in Learning

The goal orientation students have for learning something is linked to the effort they expend and their approach to learning.

Students who approach learning with mastery goals tend to
be more engaged in the task
and to use better (deeper) study
strategies, thereby processing
the information more thoroughly than students motivated
predominately by performance
goals (Anderman, Austin, &
Johnson, 2002; Pugh, Linnen-
brink-Garcia, Koskey, Stewart, & Manzey, 2010). Students with
performance goals tend to use surface study strategies that might
allow them to get a good grade on tests or quizzes but contribute little to conceptual understanding (Meece, Anderman, & Anderman,
2006) or deep engagement (Pugh et al., 2010). The very nature of
scientific advancement depends on having individuals establish a
repertoire of well-developed knowledge that subsequent learning
can be built upon and a deep understanding that can lead to the
type of questioning and connections that drive scientific progress.
For that reason alone, a mastery goal orientation is worth trying to
foster in science students.

Rdecom

Performance Goals Do Not
Promote Optimal Academic Dispositions

Students with strong performance approach goals generally
want to do well academically, but they also tend to adopt some dis-
positions that do not bode well for learning science. For example,
students who hold performance approach goals tend to play it safe
in their coursework. They are focused on looking smart, so they
would rather invest themselves in getting easy points and sidestep
challenges. While that might give them an edge on a timed test, it
also runs the risk of curtailing the development of the tenacity
necessary to meet challenges and to learn from failure, which is so
essential to science. The historical record is rife with examples of
scientists such as Darwin, Edison, and Pasteur, who failed initially
at school, careers, or inventions and yet ended up advancing scientific progress because they did not give up (Pajares, n.d.).

Students who hold strong performance avoidance goals tend
to respond to failure by adopting what is called a *helpless orientation* (where they don't believe they have the ability to succeed and

thus give up on trying altogether) or by procrastinating (Meece et al., 2006). The underlying logic behind procrastination is that if the student does not try or puts off doing work, then poor performance or even failure can be explained away by blaming bad habits rather than low ability. Obviously, teachers want their students to persist rather than give up. Performance avoidance goals are particularly detrimental to the effort and academic success of students who believe that they lack the ability to succeed (the helpless orientation), so teachers will want to be aware of the possible interaction of goal orientation and ability beliefs (Kaplan & Maehr, 2007; see also Chapter 8).

Goal Orientation Is Linked to Academic Outcomes

Goal orientation is also linked to how well students do in the long run. Goal orientation has been linked to students' cognitive processing (Anderman & Sinatra, 2009), grades, and self-perceptions (Anderman & Wolters, 2006). Furthermore, young scientists who primarily hold mastery goals tend to be more productive than those who primarily hold performance goals (Hazari, Potvin, Tai, & Almarode, 2010).

Performance Goals Are Not All Bad

Most motivation experts have advocated developing mastery goal orientation while mitigating performance goal orientation. Performance goals play a role, however, in motivating students to amass the credentials they need to advance in science classes. If students cared only about learning things but not about getting good grades or test scores, then they might not turn in their assignments on time, or they might spend all their time on an assignment worth 1 percent of their grade and blow off an assignment worth 25 percent of their grade. Consequently, although they might know the most about science or understand concepts deeply, they will not have the requirements necessary for admission into higher-level courses or the best colleges. This has led some experts to conclude that it is worthwhile for a student to have both mastery and performance approach goals (Barron & Harackiewicz, 2001), an argument we endorse here for its practical value.

Teachers Can Influence Students' Goal Orientations

Another reason that goal orientation is important for science teachers is that teachers' practices and their classroom design influence students' goal orientation. Teachers who understand goal orientation can consciously design classrooms to promote optimal student motivation (Meece et al., 2006). It is important for teachers to learn about goal orientation and about how they can impact this important aspect of student motivation.

WHAT HAVE RESEARCHERS DISCOVERED ABOUT GOALS IN SCIENCE CLASSROOMS?

Students Adopt Goal Structures Promoted in Their Classrooms

An enduring and critically important finding from empirical studies of motivation within high school science classrooms is that the classroom structures designed by teachers and the discourse that teachers engage in with their students influence whether students adopt a mastery goal orientation or a performance goal orientation (Anderman & Sinatra, 2009). Not surprisingly, a mastery goal orientation is fostered in high school science classrooms where mastery goals are valued and promoted. The students in such classrooms adopt study habits that lead them to process content deeply; they will monitor their comprehension, reorganize new information they encounter, and make connections to prior knowledge in such classrooms (Anderman & Young, 1994; Nolen & Haladyna, 1990). Alternatively, if their science teachers focus on ability by calling attention to the "best" students, mastery goal orientation declines and students tend to utilize surface-level study strategies (Anderman & Young, 1994).

Science Classrooms Tend to Emphasize Performance Goals

The teachers in the Science-in-the-Moment (SciMo) study generally structured their classrooms with a heavy reliance on performance goal orientation compared to mastery goal orientation

(Zaleski, 2012). For example, we observed teachers frequently admonishing their students to complete their work in order to obtain points and receive good grades rather than explaining why it was important to learn the material. The end point seemed to be the grade rather than interest, application, or even understanding of the material (see Chapter 2 on value for more detail). In addition, we saw very little fostering of mastery goal orientation through the encouragement of deep-learning strategies. None of the labs we observed used the inquiry method, students were almost never asked to engage in problem solving or critical thinking, and content was taught as fact with little explanation involving *why or how* (Shumow, Lyutykh, & Schmidt, 2011). The inquiry method is compatible with (and encourages) a mastery goal orientation and is related to students' self-regulation of their learning (Velayutham, Aldridge, & Fraser, 2012).

Most Students Do Not Hold Strong Mastery Goals for Science

Student participants in the SciMo study provided several types of information related to mastery and performance goals, and our data suggest that these students do not have especially strong mastery goals for science. On one survey, about 50 percent of the students reported that they would like to understand more about scientific explanations, yet only about 25 percent of them were interested in studying science more deeply. Although about 66 percent of the students reported that their teacher made sure that they understood the goals of the class and what they needed to do, 66 percent of the students also believed that it was unlikely that they would actually achieve those goals; only 16.6 percent reported that it was likely, with an additional 17.9 percent reporting that it was somewhat likely that they would be able to achieve their goals in the class. The Experience Sampling Method (ESM) data shed additional light on students' perspectives regarding whether they were learning, working hard, or feeling competitive. As shown in Table 7.1, students did not feel competitive often, so performance approach goals were not evident. In terms of how often students perceived that they were learning/improving or that they were working hard, the mean of both of those student reports fell a bit below "somewhat." Composite engagement variables indicated that students also were slightly less than "somewhat" engaged during their high school science classes. Situations where performance was emphasized led to less reported learning, enjoyment, and cooperation as well as greater stress.

Table 7.1   Indicators of Students' Goal Orientation in Science

	Learning or Improving (%)	Working Hard (%)	Feeling Competitive (%)
Not at All (0)	14.6	12.4	72.9
A Little (1)	24.8	22.8	13.7
Somewhat (2)	37.8	36.7	8.8
Very Much (3)	22.9	28.8	4.6
Mean (Standard Deviation)	1.69 (.98)	1.8 (.98)	.45 (.84)

Teachers May Believe That Boys and Girls Have Different Goal Orientations

The SciMo teachers perceived that female students were more driven by grades and more careful to fulfill stated requirements than male students, suggesting that (in the teachers' experience) female students, especially those who were successful, evinced more of a performance goal orientation. On the other hand, the teachers thought that the successful male students were more driven by interest and curiosity, suggesting that they were mastery goal oriented. Interestingly, given that the most successful students are high in both mastery goal orientations and performance approach orientations, none of the teachers described successful students who had both. A different study, retrospectively focused on the high school physics experience of college students in an introductory class (Hazari, Tai, & Sadler, 2007), suggested that high school teachers can be successful with female students by emphasizing a deep understanding of the topics and utilizing a teaching strategy aligned with mastery goal orientation. Emphasizing deeper understanding benefitted female students more than male students.

When the Classroom Is Mastery Focused, Students Use Better Strategies

Experts on student motivation argue that it is important for teachers to promote mastery goals in their students. A powerful reason they offer to support that argument is that if students perceive that their teacher emphasizes learning over performance, students will employ academic strategies that enable them to understand the material more deeply. The end result is that students in mastery-focused classrooms are more likely to be organized and diligent in their classwork (Urdan & Midgley, 2003).

Parent Involvement Promotes Mastery Orientation

Research has found that parents play a pivotal role in students' goal orientations (Frome & Eccles, 1998). Gonzalez, Doan Holbein, and Quilter (2002) showed that the more parents were involved with their high school students, the more likely students were to have a mastery goal orientation. They found similar positive effects of parental homework monitoring, parental involvement at school, and parents' knowledge about what was going on at school on mastery goal orientation.

HOW CAN TEACHERS INFLUENCE STUDENTS' GOAL ORIENTATION?

High schools tend to be organized in ways that promote performance goals far more than mastery goals, so most teachers have experience and have developed skills related to promoting performance goals, especially performance approach goals. Consequently, this section will focus more on how to increase mastery goal orientation. Because simultaneously having both mastery goals and performance approach goals is likely to be the most adaptive pattern for student success (Barron & Harackiewicz, 2001), this section will also present ideas for how to avert some of the negative outcomes associated with performance goals.

Structure Class Activities and Routines to Promote a Mastery Goal Orientation

The inquiry approach, which has been promoted extensively in the science education field because of its consistency with the nature of science, has the added benefit of being mastery goal oriented (Anderman & Sinatra, 2009). An explication of the inquiry approach is beyond the scope of this chapter, but we urge science teachers to hone their skills in that approach and refer you to the myriad resources available within your discipline and professional organizations for designing inquiry approaches to curriculum. Several books on this topic are also listed on our website, in the references associated with the chapter on autonomy (Chapter 4).

Students who are involved in active learning are likely to increase their mastery goal orientation. High school science teachers can engage students by asking questions, eliciting widespread student participation by calling on all students, and including two or more types of activities (e.g., discussion, presentation, seatwork, lab work, small-group work) during each class period (Anderman, Andrzejewski, & Allen, 2011). It is especially important for teachers to ask higher-order or elaborative questions that require more than a regurgitation of facts. Responses that should become commonplace include How do you know that? Why? Can you explain that? How is that like *x?* What would happen if *y?* Who can elaborate on or show that?

Teachers need access to what their students know in order to plan instruction that will maximize students' learning. Formative assessments and pretests are valuable tools and can include both knowledge and attitude questions. Researchers have noted that student perceptions of the goal orientation of a classroom are more predictive of their learning behavior than are teacher perceptions of the mastery goal orientation they establish. Therefore, it is advisable for teachers to gather students' perceptions of the goal structure of their classroom and on the students' goal orientation as part of any formative assessment that is done of students' knowledge (Anderman & Sinatra, 2009).

Mastery goal oriented students are more likely to endorse and use effective and deep processing study strategies, which can be taught and learned (Pintrich, 2000). Deep processing strategies include reorganizing information, monitoring comprehension, and relating content to prior knowledge (Nolen & Haladyna, 1990). These strategies take time and effort, so students need encouragement to use those strategies and to recognize how much more they learn when they use them. High school science teachers who incorporate the use of study strategies and who help their students to use such strategies promote mastery goals and a deeper understanding of science content. One way to highlight and encourage comprehension monitoring is to expect, respond to, and reinforce student questions about and connections to new content (Anderman et al., 2011). All questions need to be recognized as positive so that students do not feel dumb for asking questions. Assignments can require students to reorganize what was presented in the text or in class by reformulating the information into another modality (e.g., a graphic) or by summarizing it in the student's own words. Students can also be asked to make connections to concepts or facts that were learned previously.

Another way of promoting mastery orientation is to foster a growth mindset (see Chapter 8) and to encourage students to seek help in order to improve. Students can be expected to monitor their own understanding and be provided with options about how to improve (see Chapter 4). For example, teachers can offer the options of coming in to get extra help, seeking help from peers, or seeking help from other resources that are made available (Anderman et al., 2011). Students can be involved in setting and monitoring their goals for learning and performance. They can chart or graph their progress, thereby tracking and monitoring their progress. When help is offered within a climate of learning from mistakes, students will be more likely to accept the help. Teachers can emphasize the value of errors for learning; help students analyze their own errors; and serve as role models by admitting that they may not know the answer, but they can find and learn the answer.

Finally, efficient use of time is central to communicating that learning and mastery are valued. Students become engaged and develop a respect for learning a subject when the teacher is well-organized and focused on the importance of using time wisely (Anderman et al., 2011). We, unfortunately, documented a considerable amount of wasted time in the classrooms that we observed (Schmidt, Zaleski, Shumow, Ochoa-Angrino, & Hamidova, 2011). In our experience, teachers must constantly and diligently monitor and protect their classes from down time at the beginning and end of each class as well as establish routines that alleviate the need for spending time giving and repeating directions.

Teachers can also preempt typical issues that waste time by identifying foreseeable bottlenecks and time sinks, especially during labs (Anderman et al., 2011).

Use Verbal Feedback and Recognition That Promotes a Mastery Orientation

There are many ways for teachers to use language and give feedback in ways that promote a mastery goal orientation. It is important to interpret mistakes and errors as an essential part of the learning process, because not only is this true with respect to learning in general, it is fundamental to scientific progress in particular. It is also helpful to recognize improvement, growth, and effort. Yet another strategy is to emphasize that the purpose of classwork and assignments is to gain a deeper understanding of the material, not just to produce a perfect product (Velayutham et al., 2012). Similarly, teachers can de-emphasize performance goals by avoiding making public comparisons to the performance of peers and classmates or emphasizing grades over learning, understanding, and effort. Figure 7.1 presents some examples of mastery-oriented and performance-oriented feedback.

Promote Mastery Through Assessment

Competitive grading practices foster and reinforce a performance goal orientation (Meece et al., 2006). Alternatively, teachers foster a mastery goal orientation when it is theoretically possible for every student to succeed if they meet the standards. This approach is very different than grading with a norm-referenced system, which presupposes that students will fall onto a bell-shaped curve. It is also recommended that teachers assess higher-order thinking in the subject and promote mastery of content (Anderman & Sinatra, 2009); if success on examinations can be achieved simply by memorizing the material, then students will have little reason to value deeper processing and learning. Giving cumulative tests will benefit both boys and girls, but it is especially important for girls, because it will reinforce the idea that students need to have a full understanding of the concepts and that memorization of isolated facts is not enough (Hazari et al., 2007).

Figure 7.1   Examples of Mastery-Oriented and Performance-Oriented Feedback

Mastery-Oriented Feedback	Performance-Oriented Feedback
"You have really learned a lot about x."	"You are so smart!"
"Look at how much better you are getting!"	"You got an A!"
"That's a productive approach!"	"Hey, everybody, look at him; do it his way"
"You have really improved at . . ."	"You got 9 of the 10 points."
"I notice you are thinking deeply; that's the way to succeed."	"That's a smart idea. No one else thought of that."
"That was your personal best, and I know you will keep improving."	"You did better than anyone!"
"I can see how hard you worked."	"It's your lucky day—a perfect score!"
"I know you are disappointed in your test score and that you did your homework and studied. I notice that you are approaching learning the material by rote—that method does not work as well for answering the higher-level questions on the test. Let's look at some more effective study methods."	"I know you are disappointed in your test score. The next unit test does not have so many higher-level questions on it. It's much easier, and I am sure your grade will go up after you take that one."
"Hmm, let's see why you did not do well. It seems you are struggling with the math, which impacted how well you did on these problems. I'll give you half of the points for each problem you redo correctly. Be sure you monitor where you went wrong as you work them through."	"Hmm, it seems you are not good at math, which is affecting your physics grade. Maybe you should switch to a different science elective next semester, like anatomy, which does not require these types of math skills."

Another assessment practice that promotes a mastery goal orientation is to give credit for student improvement (Meece et al., 2006). There are several ways to do this. Some teachers allow students to correct their mistakes on tests or assignments for additional credit (the amount of that credit should be decided by each teacher); the corrections can be accompanied by an explanation of why the initial answer was wrong. This practice reinforces the notion, central to a mastery goal orientation, that mistakes are a necessary part of the learning process. Other systems focusing on improvement include giving bonus points to students who get questions right on posttests that were wrong on their pretest or giving extra points to students who improve their average grade in class (Slavin, 2000). The savvy high school teacher will want to be aware of and avoid the possibility that high school students might try to game the system by purposefully getting low pretest scores. After quizzes and tests are over, it can be useful to have students chart and compare their performance relative to whether they used surface or deep study strategies.

To emphasize that the purpose of homework is to promote understanding rather than to rack up points toward a grade, teachers can de-emphasize or even eliminate the point values associated with homework assignments and other activities intended to give students the opportunity to practice. Some teachers that we know require effective homework completion in order for students to take tests and other assessments that count toward their grade, but do not assign specific points for homework. This way, students learn that homework is a safe way for them to explore their thoughts and practice their skills and that this leads to learning.

Closely Monitor Grouping Practices

In many cases, ability grouping can reinforce a performance goal orientation, because students become focused on performing well enough on assessments to either get into a higher group or avoid being in the lowest group (Meece et al., 2006). Most of us can remember the fear and shame associated with the prospect of being in the low group: This preoccupation takes the focus away from learning. Having students collaborate in mixed-ability cooperative groups is recommended as a way of promoting learning goals (Anderman & Sinatra, 2009). Peer relationships and cooperative groups are discussed in Chapter 3. The skillful teacher can employ ability grouping flexibly, in a way that does not necessarily promote a performance goal orientation. When done correctly, differentiating content by readiness provides students with an appropriate level of challenge through flexible grouping, which may foster deeper engagement in content. For a guide to effectively differentiating by skill level in high school classrooms, the reader is referred to a guidebook developed by Tomlinson and Strickland (2005). We also discuss differentiation again in Chapter 9.

Develop Positive Teacher-Student Relationships

High-mastery classrooms are characterized by positive teacher-student relationships and interactions; such relationship patterns have not been observed in low-mastery classrooms. Teacher-student relationships are discussed in Chapter 3.

Involve Parents

The research of Gonzalez and colleagues (2002) suggests that teachers can take several routes to encouraging parent involvement that might be helpful in furthering mastery goal orientation in students. First, the resources provided to support homework completion in both the autonomy and success sections of our website (corresponding to Chapters 4 and 6 in the book) could be made available to parents, with the suggestion that they promote the use of those tools. Second, parents can be invited to attend school events such as open houses or science fairs related to science class. Third, parents can be kept informed about the goals of the science class that focus on learning and mastery goals and on their child's progress toward reaching those goals. It can be helpful to explain to parents directly why mastery goal orientation is important and to emphasize mastery goals for each unit. This can be done relatively easily through periodic e-mails or posts on a class website that parents can access. A handout for parents is available on our website; the handout can be linked to your own webpage or distributed during open house, conferences, or through other venues that provide opportunities for parent-teacher communication.

WHAT RESOURCES CAN SCIENCE TEACHERS USE TO FOSTER ADAPTIVE GOAL ORIENTATIONS?

The companion website, http://www.niu.edu/eteams, contains useful resources that can be helpful to teachers as they work to promote effective goal orientations in their classroom or that can be recommended for parents of their students. The following and more can be found on the website:

- Checklists for identifying performance goal oriented and mastery goal oriented classrooms
- Links to websites that provide information on study and self-regulatory skills
- Guides for creating mastery goal oriented classrooms
- Handouts on goal orientation for parents
- Streaming video clips demonstrating the strategies discussed in this chapter
- Links to publications and instruments related to goal orientation theory in classrooms

CHAPTER EIGHT

Ability Beliefs

As Ms. Ullman is discussing station models in her third-period earth science class, many of the students look confused. Pablo mutters to himself, "I'll never get this no matter what I do or how often she explains this, so why bother?" Across the room, Natalia says, "Wow, I'm totally lost, I'm gonna read that part again; maybe then I'll get it."

WHAT ARE ABILITY BELIEFS?

Ability beliefs contribute to the choices students make about studying, course taking, and careers. Common sense and empirical research tell us that students who believe they are highly able will be more motivated and will do better academically than those who believe they have low ability (see our discussion of this in Chapter 6). The research that informs this chapter, however, shows in a very compelling fashion that the equation is not that simple. In fact, this research suggests that students' perceptions of their own ability as high or low may matter less than their beliefs about the nature of ability in general or society's stereotyped beliefs about the ability of people in the social and demographic groups to which students belong. In this chapter, we will consider how mindset and stereotype threat impact students' motivation for science.

Mindset

Carol Dweck (2006b), a renowned Stanford psychologist, and her colleagues have spent years studying how people think about their abilities and how these beliefs impact motivation, learning, and achievement. Her research suggests that whether students think of their ability as fundamentally fixed or changeable (a concept she calls *mindset*) may be even more important than whether they believe their ability is high or low.

Individuals with a *fixed mindset* believe that ability is given, that it is static, unchangeable, and out of an individual's control (Dweck, 1999). A person with a fixed mindset believes we are endowed with a certain amount of ability, and that's all we get. Students who say things such as, "I'm just not good at physics" or "I'm a genius at biology" or "I'm dumb" are expressing fixed mindsets. Notice that the student who characterized herself as a genius in the field of biology, which might seem like a good thing to many biology teachers, nevertheless has a fixed mindset. Mindset is not about whether you think you have high or low ability; it's about whether you think your ability can change.

Individuals with a growth mindset believe that ability can be developed; they see intelligence as malleable, changeable, and within their control (Dweck, 1999). The student who says, "It's not that I'm a genius, I just worked really hard on this" after winning a science fair award sounds like a student with a growth mindset, as does the student who says, "I really bombed that chemistry test, but what can I expect? I played video games last night instead of studying."

Stereotype Threat

Stereotype threat (Steele & Aronson, 1995) is a form of fixed mindset that comes into play for students who identify with groups whose performance is thought to be subpar. For example, girls are often thought to be less suited for the physical sciences than boys, and African Americans are thought to be less academically successful than their White peers. Stereotype threat kicks in when students are engaged in a challenging task and poor performance on the task would confirm the negative stereotype that exists about their group. The possibility of being personally responsible for confirming a negative stereotype about a group to which one belongs creates anxiety and fear, undermines motivation, and affects performance. High school students are impacted by stereotypes and bias regardless of whether these harmful beliefs have been expressed explicitly or implicitly. Research demonstrates that stereotype threat operates for girls in science, technology, engineering, and math (STEM) subjects (Nguyen & Ryan, 2008; Spencer, Steele, & Quinn, 1999) and for racial and ethnic minority groups in many academic subjects (Aronson & Good, 2003; Aronson, Quinn, & Spencer, 1998; Steele, 1997).

WHY ARE ABILITY BELIEFS IMPORTANT?

Students' ability beliefs profoundly impact their effort, study skills, and subsequent success as learners and also shape their career choices. The evidence shows that mindset beliefs influence students' choice of college coursework and their academic success in middle school, high school, and college (Blackwell, Trzesniewski, & Dweck, 2007; Mangels, Good, Whiteman, Maniscalco, & Dweck, 2012; Nguyen & Ryan, 2008; Rydell, Shiffrin, Boucher, Van Loo, & Rydell, 2010).

The Academic Behaviors Associated With a Growth Mindset Are More Desirable

Figure 8.1 illustrates the types of student behaviors that are typically associated with holding a growth or a fixed mindset (Holmes, 2002). The behaviors associated with a fixed mindset are generally all responses that science teachers would rather their students avoid. The opposite is true for the behaviors associated with having a growth mindset—teachers want their students to adopt those behaviors, because experienced educators know that those approaches are the signs of a motivated student and are likely to result in more learning. The reader will notice that students with a fixed mindset tend to have goals that focus on performance, whereas those with a growth mindset tend to be focused on learning (see Chapter 7 for more information about goal orientation). Given the attitudes and approaches to learning adopted by students with a growth mindset, it is not surprising that these students are more successful when compared to students with fixed mindsets.

Figure 8.1   Fixed and Growth Mindsets Compared

	Fixed Mindset	Growth Mindset
Reaction to Challenge	Avoids challenge in order to look smart	Embraces challenges in order to learn
Persistence	Gives up easily	Persists despite obstacles
Approach to Effort	Sees effort as futile	Sees effort as way to succeed
Response to Feedback	Ignores useful feedback	Learns from feedback
Response to Success of Others	Threatened by others' success	Inspired by others' success
Attributions for Failure	Lack of ability	Insufficient effort or strategies

Girls and Boys May Be Socialized to Have Different Mindsets

Dweck (2006a) suggests that bright girls may be particularly vulnerable to the negative effects of having a fixed mindset. These girls have been academically successful their whole lives and have been praised for their accomplishments by well-meaning adults who tell them repeatedly, "You are so smart!" This well-intentioned praise, coupled with relatively effortless academic success solidifies a fixed mindset in which these girls believe, "Yes, I am one of the smart ones." The problem arises when these young women face the significant academic challenges they will inevitably encounter in higher-level science classes. When this occurs, a student may question her identity as one of the "smart ones." She then concludes that since success did not come to her easily, she must not have what it takes; she has reached the limit of her ability. These students subsequently give up on the task at precisely the moment they should be expending the most effort.

The story looks different for boys. Because boys tend to be more physically active in childhood, they are often perceived by teachers as being less compliant, even if they are academically successful. As a result, the message young boys tend to get from teachers and parents are something along these lines: "I know you can do this, you just have to apply yourself." When these male students encounter academic challenges, this same message kicks in: "You just have to try harder, and then you will get it." So the way that teachers and parents traditionally support and encourage boys' and girls' education may actually promote a more fixed mindset among girls and a stronger growth mindset among boys, particularly in areas such as science, where gender stereotypes exist (Dweck, 1999). We have seen this scenario play out in our own research in science classrooms and find that it resonates very deeply with many of the young women and men we encounter in our college classrooms.

Scientists Need a Growth Mindset

The very nature of science depends on being able to embrace the challenges of learning new knowledge, to persist in the face of obstacles, to correct errors, and to respond to feedback from peers. Scientists often fail when they are doing experiments, and they use that failure to learn. A growth mindset, then, is consistent with acting and thinking like a scientist.

Stereotype Threat Can Be Damaging

It is essential for teachers to be aware of how stereotype threat operates, because the damage that results from the anxiety and fear of confirming negative stereotypes can be great, hindering performance and reducing motivation. Students who perceive stereotype threat will not do as well as other students or even as well as they themselves do under conditions where stereotype threat is removed (Purdie-Vaughns, 2012). Unless efforts are made to reduce or overcome stereotype threat, students from groups that are believed to be less capable (e.g., women in physics or engineering) are likely to underperform and abandon those areas for other pursuits.

Beyond teachers' natural desire for their students to learn and achieve, external pressures heighten the costs of stereotype threat. The national need for well-trained scientists and engineers is compelling; fulfilling that need requires that women and other underrepresented groups be prepared to succeed in STEM careers (Rodriguez, 2012; Suresh, 2012). Additionally, schools are now being held accountable for the performance of traditionally stigmatized groups on standardized assessments, and there has been pressure to use student scores on those measures in teacher evaluations. Luckily, teachers and other important adults can foster growth mindsets and reduce both fixed mindsets and stereotype threats. Ability beliefs develop in response to experience, and they can be changed.

WHAT HAVE RESEARCHERS DISCOVERED ABOUT ABILITY BELIEFS IN SCIENCE CLASSROOMS?

Mindset Matters for Science Achievement and Persistence

While there is a good deal of evidence that having a growth mindset promotes academic achievement in general (see Dweck, 1999, 2006b for reviews), there are a handful of studies demonstrating that mindset may be especially relevant for achievement and persistence in STEM fields in particular. Several decades ago, Williams and King (1980) provided evidence that math skills are more likely to be viewed as fixed compared to skills in other subject areas. Additionally, Dweck and colleagues found that middle school students who have a growth mindset when it comes to math were more likely to show increases in math achievement over time compared to students with a fixed mindset (Hill, Corbett, & St. Rose, 2010). Math is, of course, foundational to science; thus the positive impacts of a growth mindset in math would likely carry over to science as well.

Mindset May Be a Cause and a Solution for Gender Gaps in Science

While mindset was not assessed directly in the Science-in-the-Moment (SciMo) Project, we observed many things to suggest that girls were more likely to have a fixed mindset than boys when it comes to science. To begin with, the girls in our study viewed themselves as having fewer science abilities than boys. While this information alone does not in itself signal a fixed mindset, it makes other evidence we gathered all the more troubling.

When we observed science classrooms, girls tended to take on a helpless orientation more often than boys, expressing the idea that they "just couldn't" do the tasks they were asked to do or making comments about the futility of their efforts in class. Most alarmingly, we were able to document with students' Experience Sampling Method (ESM) reports that as soon as science instruction became challenging, girls disengaged and backed away from the activity, while boys jumped right in (these findings are presented in graphic form in Figure 9.3). The reader will recall that backing away from challenge is one of the hallmarks of a fixed mindset and stems from the belief that effort is a waste of time if one's ability can't change. Girls' beliefs that they are not good at science, coupled with the notion that they never will be good, may deliver the proverbial one-two punch for girls' future motivation and persistence in science.

Research suggests that having a growth mindset might protect girls from gender gaps in performance and promote persistence in STEM subject areas (Good, Aronson, & Inzlicht, 2003; Good et al., 2009 as cited in Hill et al., 2010; Grant & Dweck, 2003). For example, women with growth mindsets show greater persistence in college-level STEM courses compared to women with fixed mindsets (Good et al., 2009 as cited in Hill et al., 2010). In studies involving junior high and college students, the researchers found that when they looked only at those students who had fixed mindsets, male students consistently outperformed female students in math and science. However, when the researchers turned their focus to those who had growth mindsets, they found no gender differences in achievement. They also found that when girls and women had a fixed mindset, they were very vulnerable to the stereotype threat that girls are not as good as boys at math. In other words, when faced with math-related challenges, these girls and women were more likely to buy into the stereotype. Conversely, girls and women with a growth mindset did not fall prey to this stereotype when they faced challenging academic tasks (Good et al., 2003).

Even more remarkably, in a study that attempted to manipulate mindset, Dweck and colleagues (Good et al., 2009 as cited in Hill et al., 2010) provided instruction to adolescents in which some students learned that accomplished mathematicians had

natural ability (a fixed mindset message) and some students learned that accomplished mathematicians struggled a lot and had to work very hard (a growth mindset message). When the students who got the fixed mindset message later took a challenging math test, boys outperformed girls. However, among the students who got the growth mindset message, there were no gender differences in performance (Hill et al., 2010).

VLADGRIN Shutterstock

When Students Understand How the Brain Works, They Develop a Growth Mindset

Researchers in neuroscience and psychology have amassed evidence supporting the wisdom of having a growth mindset—the human brain does change in response to experience and people do become more skilled and intelligent as a result of learning (Posner & Rothbart, 2007). When adolescents are aware that the brain works in this way, they tend to become more motivated and focus on learning and effort rather than on looking smart, a conclusion substantiated by experimental research. This research demonstrated that changing students' mindset actually changes their levels of achievement and learning. Students who participated in educational interventions designed to develop growth mindsets by teaching them about brain growth and study strategies improved far more academically in comparison to a control group of students who learned only study strategies (Blackwell et al., 2007).

In countering the fixed mindset associated with stereotype threat, it is important to understand how stereotype threat operates (Schmader, Johns, & Forbes, 2008). First, students experiencing stereotype threat are stressed by it, which interferes with their cognitive processing. Second, students who perceive stereotype threat often get into a vicious cycle of monitoring themselves, hypervigilance, and anxiety. Third, some students focus their energy on tamping down their negative thoughts and emotions rather than learning the content. All of these reactions sap the mental resources and interfere with the thought processes that students need to do well in school.

Even Well-Meaning Teachers Have Biases That May Contribute to Students' Perceptions of Stereotype Threat and Development of a Fixed Mindset

One of the things we discovered from interviewing high school science teachers is that few of them explicitly endorsed stereotypes about girls or other underrepresented groups in science. Teachers know that such stereotypes are wrong, and they are dedicated to teaching and helping all their students succeed. Nevertheless, a lifetime of exposure to stereotypes does leave some residue—we found that many high school science teachers who explicitly disavowed stereotypes did express stereotypes implicitly when we asked them to talk about their own students. Furthermore, a considerable number of teachers acted on these stereotypes in their classrooms (Shumow, Schmidt, & Darfler, 2010). As we mentioned in Chapter 1, teachers addressed their male students more often than they addressed their female students. This behavior suggests that teachers may not even be aware that their practices reflect a belief that male students are more able to engage in science in this way or are more interested.

There Are Several Different Ways to Alleviate Stereotype Threat

In an analysis of many different studies, Nguyen and Ryan (2008) discovered that female students responded best to very explicit approaches to removing stereotype threat. Examples of approaches that were effective for girls and women include teaching directly about stereotype threat and making explicit statements that tests are free of bias. They found that more subtle approaches to removing stereotype threat seemed to work best among students from other underrepresented groups such as racial and ethnic minorities. Examples of more subtle approaches to removing stereotype threat include de-emphasizing the importance of tests by saying "It won't count for much" or by providing students access to successful role models from their racial or ethnic group. The take-away message from this research is that teachers can do a great deal to remove potential stereotype threat in their classrooms and that using a variety of approaches might be advisable, since different approaches seem to be more effective for different groups of students.

HOW CAN TEACHERS FOSTER ABILITY BELIEFS CONDUCIVE TO SUCCESS IN SCIENCE?

Praise Effort, Not Ability

We have heard many high school science teachers positively respond to students who answer a simple question quickly by saying, "You are *so* smart!" Of course, the teachers mean well, but what happens psychologically as a result of such praise when a student does not know the answer quickly or when the problem requires effort? The very real danger is that they will interpret the need to reflect or to struggle as meaning that they are not smart. In this framework, having to expend effort is seen as a glaring, flashing indicator of low ability. While this sounds counterintuitive, simply telling a student that he or she is smart may actually lead to very harmful beliefs about the nature of ability, which could get in the way of future academic success. Rather than praising ability, teachers can praise hard work and tenacity, being sure to give students the message that effort is how people learn. Dweck (2002, 2007) also recommends telling students who are able to complete their work quickly and with little effort something similar to, "You seem to have mastered this and can do with more challenging material; let's find some for you." She also suggests that teachers tell students that they want them to be challenged rather than waste time dwelling on content that is too easy.

Teach about Brain Development

Tell students that learning, studying, and practice actually increase intelligence. Teachers can foster a growth mindset by teaching the science of brain development and malleability, explaining how the brain forms new connections and actually gets heavier as people learn. Our companion website contains many helpful resources for teaching this content. The Brainology Program—an interactive, web-based computer program with associated offline lessons, activities, and teacher education materials—was developed by Dweck, Blackwell, and colleagues to foster a growth mindset (see resources section on companion website). This program contains lessons that expose adolescents to the science of how the brain responds to learning and experience. We have used this program ourselves and have observed that students are quite surprised to learn this information and readily come to appreciate the ways they can take control over their ability.

Teach Students How to Learn

Students who adopt a growth mindset will be more open to learning and using study strategies that will help them improve their ability. They need to be challenged and praised for effort, but they also need the tools and strategies to learn. Incorporating study strategies into one's classroom and applying them during test preparation are excellent ways to help students succeed. Instruction in the use of study strategies is much more effective if it is embedded within course content, as we suggest here, rather than taught as a separate unit or course (Wingate, 2006). Those students who try hard but still do not succeed need to hear the message that their effort is good but will be more successful if they use deep study strategies. Importantly, as noted earlier, teaching study strategies has a far greater impact when combined with teaching about brain changes related to learning.

Highlight the Struggle

Struggling is often part of the process of learning, but few students understand that without guidance. The way teachers respond to errors gives students powerful messages about persistence and challenge. A teacher can embrace errors enthusiastically by telling students that they offer an opportunity to learn. Saying things such as, "This happens all the time in real labs, too. Let's figure out what went wrong," helps students learn to accept setbacks as part of the process of doing science and to overcome the inevitable obstacles they will encounter in learning and accomplishing complex tasks. Teachers can also talk about struggles they have encountered and resolved.

Look Out for Gifted Students With Fixed Mindsets

We have encountered teachers who mistake having a growth mindset with giftedness. Actually, these are not interchangeable. The very act of labeling students as *gifted* runs the same risk as praising intelligence (Dweck, 2002). A fixed mindset can hold a high achiever back, as noted earlier in our discussion of bright girls; it might behoove educators to be aware of that and to address it using some of the five teaching practices represented in Figure 8.2.

Try to Reduce Stereotype Threat

A number of techniques have been demonstrated to reduce stereotype threat (Nguyen & Ryan, 2008; Purdie-Vaughns, 2012). Those techniques that can reasonably be applied in a classroom setting are represented in Figure 8.2.

Wise feedback is a way of providing critical feedback in a way that does not increase stereotype threat or imply a fixed mindset message. Wise feedback combines clear, constructive feedback about what is wrong and needs to be improved with a statement indicating that the teacher has high expectations and believes that the student can, in fact, meet those high expectations. For example, science teachers giving wise feedback might say something such as, "You missed nearly all the items pertaining to cell division. You were absent for most classes on this topic. When that happens, I expect you to study those concepts or sections in the textbook thoroughly on your own and review the posted materials. You need to check your understanding on the review items with your lab partner and come in before or after school for help if you do not understand it completely. I'm telling you this, because I think you

Figure 8.2 Techniques That Reduce Stereotype Threat

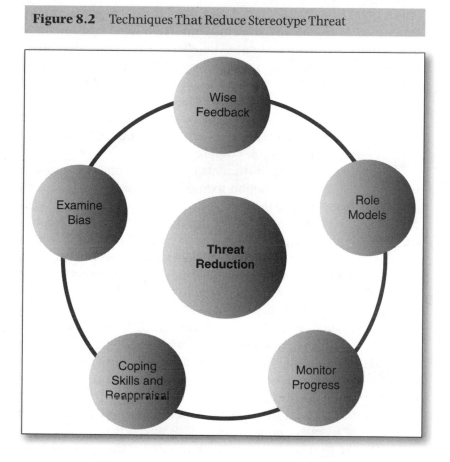

can meet the high standards in this class. If I did not think you could do it, I would not make the effort to give you this feedback." Another example of wise feedback is "This graph does not represent the data properly. Please redo it, using the guide about graphing different types of data in the appendix of your lab book, and ask me questions if you are unsure. I do expect a lot in the lab reports, but I am sure that you can meet those expectations."

Calling attention to role models also can help to reduce stereotype threat (Halpern et al., 2007; Nguyen & Ryan, 2008; Purdie-Vaughns, 2012). Science teachers can call attention to female scientists or scientists from other underrepresented groups who have accomplished great things. Teachers can ask students to write or talk about the contributions of these individuals and to reflect upon how they broke through any barriers to achievement. Experimental studies suggest that taking about 10 minutes to do this activity just once can have the effect of reducing stereotype threat for an entire year. Another, more subtle way to call attention to role models is to display posters and pictures of female and ethnic minority scientists in the classroom (Inzlicht, Tullett, Legault, & Kang, 2011). The reader can refer to the confidence section of our companion website (corresponding to Chapter 5) to find resources for finding role models.

Teachers can help their students by teaching and encouraging the use of cognitive and emotion-focused coping skills, such as reappraisal and mindfulness (Inzlicht et al., 2011). *Reappraisal* is a cognitive coping skill that involves redefining a demanding situation (such as a test) as being challenging rather than threatening, which introduces an entirely different physiological response. For example, seeing a test as threatening evokes fear or anxiety whereas seeing it as challenging can evoke positive emotions. This technique might work better for male students than female students (see Chapter 9 for more on challenge). *Mindfulness interventions* have also been used successfully to help students cope with emotional responses to stressful situations. Mindfulness approaches include simple breathing and meditation techniques (see the companion website for resources on mindfulness).

It is important for teachers to examine their own biases. The more aware teachers are of their beliefs and practices, the more able they are to take steps to realize the egalitarian goals that so many of them express. Some teachers have taken steps to monitor their interaction with male and female students by having a colleague observe them and collect data on their interaction patterns. Other teachers use systems to call on students (such as drawing names written on tongue depressors or craft sticks or keeping a class roster with response tallies) to ensure that they do not call on male students more than female students.

Finally, teachers will need to monitor how well any of these approaches are working for their students. Given that Nguyen and Ryan (2008) found that girls and students from other underrepresented groups seemed to respond differently to explicit and subtle stereotype threat removal strategies, as you try these strategies, be sure to look for indications of whether or not they work. Even though many of the approaches suggested here are not time consuming, time is of the essence in high school classrooms. Every minute does count, and it is not productive to use approaches that do not work for your students.

WHAT RESOURCES CAN SCIENCE TEACHERS USE TO UNDERSTAND AND PROMOTE GROWTH MINDSET AND REDUCE STEREOTYPE THREAT?

The companion website, http://www.niu.edu/eteams, contains helpful resources to aid teachers in promoting a growth mindset in their students and reduce stereotype threat in the science classroom. The resources can also be recommended to parents. The following and more can be found on the website:

- Articles for teachers and parents
- Links to the Brainology Program and mindset website
- Links to resources for teaching about the brain
- Links to mindfulness exercises
- Streaming video clips of scientists talking about stereotype threat and of classroom activities that promote a growth mindset
- Tools to assess mindset as well as gender and science stereotypes

CHAPTER NINE

Challenge

"Today, we are making butter!" announces Mr. Walker enthusiastically to his 9th-grade general science class. He proceeds to pass out small zip-seal plastic bags into which he pours heavy whipping cream and 2 marbles. He instructs his students, who are working in groups, to shake their sealed bags vigorously in order to separate the liquid from the solid and make butter. For the next 15 minutes, students shake their bags, socializing and laughing with their group mates. While students enjoy the butter they made on some crackers, Mr. Walker explains that that there are many different kinds of mixtures and that when students shook the cream, the marbles knocked into the molecules and separated the liquid from the fat. Sheila, who has been laughing and joking with her friends all period, comments, "This is the dumbest class ever. I hate this."

Sheila has spent the entire class laughing and socializing with her friends, doing a task that she was able to complete easily and that allowed her to stand up and move about the classroom. So why does she hate the class? She is frustrated at missing the opportunity to stretch her mind—she feels cheated of challenge.

WHAT IS CHALLENGE?

Webster's New World Dictionary defines *challenge* as "anything that requires special effort." Mihaly Csikszentmihalyi (1990), a world-renowned psychologist who has studied challenge for more than 40 years, refers to challenge as an opportunity for action or involvement that requires appropriate skills to realize. In short, a challenge is anything that requires an investment of effort, whether it is cognitive, physical, or emotional. Very often in our everyday lives, the word *challenge* has a negative connotation—as in the case of "challenging economic times," "challenging circumstances," or "this student is a real challenge"—all of which suggest things that are hard in a way that is decidedly unpleasant. In the sense that we are using it in this chapter, however, challenge is not, by definition, unpleasant. As a matter of fact, many scholars argue that challenge is precisely the ingredient that is necessary to get students excited about and engaged in academic tasks. It also allows student growth and learning to occur.

WHY IS CHALLENGE IMPORTANT?

Challenging Activities Can Be Enjoyable and Therefore Intrinsically Motivating

Researchers and theorists alike have argued that humans of all ages across the globe tend to experience the greatest enjoyment when they are involved in activities that require some investment of skill or effort (Csikszentmihalyi, 1990; Deci, 1975; Harter, 2009; White, 1959). This affective dimension of science learning is described more fully in Chapter 10. Despite many popular portrayals of adolescents as lazy, research tells us that by and large, teenagers prefer activities in which they have to invest a little bit of themselves to those they can just coast through like couch potatoes. If given the choice, many adolescents will opt for an activity that presents a moderate challenge over one that is mindless, because the challenging one is actually more enjoyable. Thus if students experience challenge in science, they may be more likely to choose to become involved in science tasks.

Challenging Activities Are More Engaging

Challenging activities are not just more enjoyable, they also require that students focus their attention and energy in engaging more deeply in the task at hand. Across a variety of subject areas, when students perceive an academic task to be challenging, they report higher levels of both concentration and interest in that task (Shernoff, Csikszentmihalyi, Schneider, & Shernoff, 2003; Shernoff & Schmidt, 2008).

USACE-Sacramento

If Students Are Not Challenged, They Are Probably Not Learning

When students are able to do all of their academic tasks without having to stretch themselves, think critically, or expend any cognitive energy, this is a sure sign that they already know the material. If, on the other hand, a task requires that students think, consult resources, and have the chance to be wrong, this is precisely where learning occurs. Challenge operates much in the same way as Vygotsky's *zone of proximal development*, which refers to a range of activities that a student cannot do alone but can do with some assistance from someone more knowledgeable or from another resource (Daniels, 2011; Vygotsky, 1962). From this perspective, intellectual development requires doing challenging tasks.

An Appropriately Challenging Task Tells Students That the Teacher Believes They Can Handle It

When a teacher challenges his or her students, students receive an implicit positive message about their abilities and the teacher's confidence in them. Academic tasks that are not challenging enough send the message to students that the teacher does not believe they can handle anything more complicated. When students succeed at tasks that they feel are challenging, they perceive themselves as becoming more competent (largely because they actually *are* becoming more competent), which in turn raises their confidence level and helps them feel as if they have more control over their own learning outcomes.

WHAT HAVE RESEARCHERS DISCOVERED ABOUT CHALLENGE IN SCIENCE CLASSROOMS?

Students Perceive Relatively Low Challenge in Science Class

It is important to emphasize here that challenge is subjective: It depends on the student's perceptions. What is most important is that the student feels challenged. Further, in the context of high school science classrooms, challenge has both cognitive and affective components. In order for a task to be perceived as challenging, a student must perceive the task as posing some degree of cognitive demand but also must recognize this demand as an opportunity for action (Baird & Penna, 1997). Interestingly, teachers may not be very good judges of whether or not their students feel challenged. Gentry, Rizza, and Owen (2002) found no correlation whatsoever between teachers' reports of the degree to which they are challenging their students and students' reports of challenge.

Our research in a variety of high school classrooms shows that challenge in science tends to be low—so low, in fact, that it was not surprising that science was not engaging to students. We asked students to report on how challenging various science tasks were while they were doing them: Looking across hundreds of students and thousands of moments in science classrooms, the average challenge rating reported by students on a scale of 0 (not at all) to 3 (very much) was 0.88. This number suggests that on average, students perceived their science activities as posing somewhere between "none" and "a little" challenge. Of the four science subject areas we studied, students consistently reported the lowest levels of challenge in biology. Students' challenge ratings in general science, chemistry, and physics classes were all about the same and were considerably higher than in biology. The challenge ratings of boys did not differ from that of girls in any of these subject areas, which suggests that observed gender gaps in science interest are not attributable to students' perceptions of challenge.

In a study of secondary science students, Baird and Penna (1997) found that students' perceptions of challenge generally declined as they moved to higher grades. Their survey results from nearly 4,000 students showed a downward trend in students' challenge ratings in science class and indicated that as students got older, more and more of them felt that they could be working harder than they were in science. This study did have an encouraging finding that is highly consistent with what motivation theory tells us about challenge as an intrinsic motivator: The researchers reported that "a significant proportion of students are dissatisfied with their current level of personal engagement in science and are willing to apply themselves harder . . . if classroom conditions and activities change" (p. 1201). In other words, if science classrooms were structured to provide more opportunities to challenge students, students indicated that they would be up for accepting the challenge.

Teachers May Misread Students' Challenge

In interviews, teachers expressed the intention of making science accessible to students: The general feeling among teachers was that students generally perceived science as hard and intimidating, so teachers often went to great lengths to soften the science so that students would not be frightened away. Our classroom observations and students' own reports of their challenge and engagement in science suggest that these well-intentioned teachers may have missed the mark: In their attempt to make science accessible, they made it too easy, and as a result, students were bored. Many students disengaged and, consequently, did not perform well on assessments. Teachers then interpreted the poor performance as an indicator that the instructional tasks they had assigned were too difficult, rather than as reflecting the low expectations they had communicated to their students through the tasks they had assigned.

How Much Challenge Is Enough?

Motivation theory tells us that there is a certain level of challenge that is optimal for facilitating student motivation (Csikszentmihalyi, 1990). Generally speaking, intermediate or moderate challenges tend to be the most motivating and engaging. When students do tasks that offer little challenge, they tend to get bored. When challenges are too high, anxiety creeps in. With intermediate challenge, students are able to become deeply engaged in an activity without experiencing anxiety and while simultaneously building their skills. Of course, the level of challenge that is optimal for a given student will depend on that student's skill level in that area. Csikszentmihalyi (1990, 1997) has written beautifully about the balance of challenge and skill in the lives of adolescents and adults and the effect of this balance on engagement, achievement, and learning. Some of these ideas are depicted in Figure 9.1.

Figure 9.1   The Impact of Challenge and Skill on Students' Engagement, Success, and Learning

| | | Challenge | |
		Low	High
Skill	High	Boredom Success with little effort is guaranteed Little learning	Optimal engagement Success is attainable, but not guaranteed Optimal learning
	Low	Apathy Success is possible, but not gratifying Little learning	Anxiety Success is unlikely Little learning

It is important for teachers to realize that the balance between challenge and skill is dynamic and constantly changing: As a student's skill develops, tasks that were once challenging eventually become easy, and there is a risk that the student can become bored. Thus it is critical to constantly monitor and adjust the difficulty level of activities as students' skills develop.

Challenge Varies by Class Activity

Because our research examined student experience during science classes, we were able to examine the level of challenge that different types of learning experiences presented to students (see Figure 9.2). The classroom activity that students rated as most

Figure 9.2 Perceived Challenge in Various Science Activities

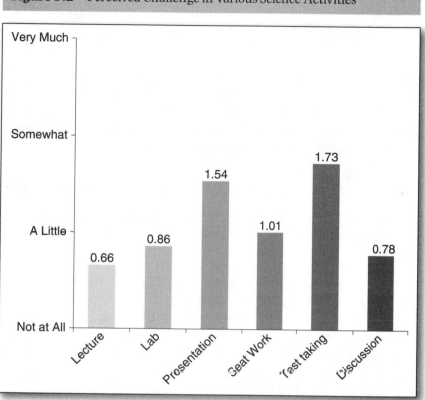

challenging was test taking. This poses sharp contrast to most other classroom activities, which were characterized as having low levels of challenge. Lab activities stand out as a particular surprise: Labs have high potential to engage and challenge students, yet this is an activity during which students reported fairly low levels of challenge (Shumow, Schmidt, & Zaleski, 2013). We speculate that the labs we observed offered so little challenge because they tended to be fairly formulaic, outlining steps much like a recipe, with an emphasis on getting the right result rather than on learning something through discovery. Students were never allowed to design and investigate their own questions or even to contemplate alternative means to answer the questions their teachers provided for them. This approach to laboratory work is particularly striking to us, as many science teachers are former scientists themselves and presumably understand that science is a process of exploration and investigation. We recognize that in today's climate of increased accountability, teachers may be pressured to teach science as an accumulation of discrete factual knowledge in order to meet standards that are measured with common local or state assessments. Unfortunately, this approach may promote an inaccurate view of science as a profession and may lead students to see science as less challenging, less interesting, and, ultimately, less appealing as a career option.

Student Response to Challenge Depends on Mindset

Up to this point, we have presented challenge as motivational: Offering students challenges is a way to get students engaged. Teachers know, however, that not all students will "take the challenge bait" with equal vigor. The work of Dweck (1999) and others reminds us that the relationship between challenge and engagement may not be so simple and may depend greatly on how students think about the nature of ability. According to Dweck, students with a *growth mindset*—those who believe that one's ability can increase with practice and effort—view challenges as opportunities to learn and increase their ability. Thus challenge is engaging for them. Conversely, students who hold a *fixed mindset*—those who believe that one's ability is fairly static and does not change much—will view a challenging activity as hard proof of their lack of ability and will back away from this challenge, seeing fewer benefits of taking this opportunity for action. The reasoning goes, "I don't know how to do this; I can't learn how to do this, so why even bother trying?" For a more thorough discussion of mindset, see Chapter 8.

Boys and Girls Respond Differently to Challenge

In our research in science classrooms, we have observed both of these patterns of engagement (or disengagement) with challenge. Sadly, girls seem to be more likely than boys to become intimidated and disengaged when they experience challenge in science. When we examine our in-the-moment reports of students' perceived challenge and engagement, we can see a pattern where among the boys, when challenge goes up, so does engagement. For girls, however, the opposite pattern is observed: As they feel more challenged, their engagement goes down (see Figure 9.3). This pattern might be due to the fact that female adolescents have lower science confidence levels than males (see Chapter 5) and/or that girls tend to have more fixed mindsets relative to boys (see Chapter 8).

Figure 9.3 High School Students' Engagement at Different Levels of Challenge

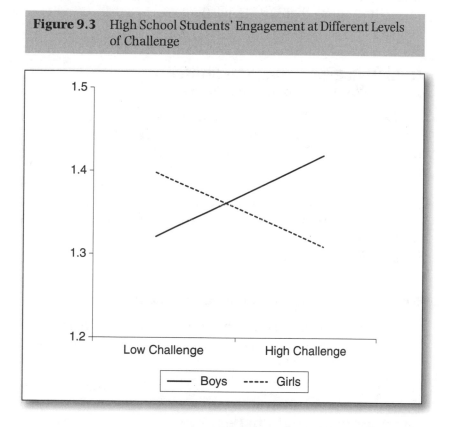

HOW CAN TEACHERS PROVIDE APPROPRIATE CHALLENGES FOR THEIR STUDENTS?

Students differ in the level of skill they bring to their science activities, in their mindset, and in the way that they will perceive challenge in the science classroom. As a result, it is unrealistic to point to a specific set of learning activities that will challenge all students. As is the case with all other aspects of educational practice, there are no magic bullets. The research provided here does suggest several important things teachers can attend to in order to most effectively assess whether they are providing appropriate challenges for their students and to encourage students to engage with challenge in ways that will promote learning and growth. While we believe the suggestions below would be beneficial for all students, they are particularly critical for female students, as our research suggests that girls in particular tend to shy away from challenges in science.

Hold High Expectations for Students, Even If Their Performance Is Low

Remember that the degree of challenge teachers provide is a reflection of their expectations and that low challenge levels communicate low expectations. If students do not think they are being challenged, they could develop the belief that their teachers do not have confidence in their abilities. Low performance on tests does not always mean that the material is over students' heads—sometimes, it means the students lost interest because they were underchallenged, and because they were not engaged, they missed content on which they were assessed later.

Present Challenge as Necessary to Learning

When a student has to expend effort on a science learning task, remind him or her that this is the only way learning happens: If one can do a task easily, one is not learning anything. As we have emphasized in other chapters, highlight the struggle.

Communicate That Challenging Tasks Are Opportunities for Action

Some students do not see challenge as presenting opportunities for action or engagement. They instead see challenges as obstacles to be avoided and abandoned. Help students see challenge as an invitation rather than a roadblock. You can model how to embrace challenge in your own problem-solving demonstrations by showing enthusiasm when students have to expend effort, by helping students choose the right strategies to move forward in their work, and by fostering metacognitive strategies to help students monitor and assess their own work (see Chapter 7 for a discussion of those strategies).

Foster a Growth Mindset

Many of the maladaptive reactions to challenge stem from a student's mindset. It is important, then, for teachers to foster a growth mindset by praising effort, teaching about the brain, highlighting the struggle, and applying the other principles we discussed in Chapter 8.

Ask Students If They Are Challenged

Science teachers should keep in mind that they may not be accurate judges of the level of challenge their students experience. When it comes to challenge, there is little relationship between what the teacher thinks he or she is doing and how the students perceive this. Teachers should ask students directly about how challenged they feel in various activities (a simple "too easy," "about right," or "too hard" type of rating will often suffice) and about how much effort students have to invest to accomplish classroom tasks. With the integration of technology into classrooms, these types of quick assessments can often be gathered in real time through the use of the clicker response systems that have become common in many high school classrooms.

Watch Out for Underchallenging as Well as Overchallenging

Our research suggests that science teachers tend to be most concerned about overwhelming their students, but the students themselves report very low levels of challenge in science.

Differentiate Instruction and Assignments

As class sizes increase, teachers are presented with a broader range of student ability and confidence. Teachers need to offer a broad range of activities and use a wide range of teaching tools in order to appropriately challenge all students. Differentiation is a very popular topic in schools these days and, if implemented with fidelity, offers promise as a tool for challenging a broad range of students without promoting potentially harmful performance goals. When teachers group students by ability, they run the risk of sending a message that emphasizes performance over learning (see Chapter 7 for a discussion of this). Truly differentiating instruction involves a cultural shift in the classroom practice that involves much more than simply grouping students by ability (Tomlinson & Strickland, 2005). A complete description of differentiated curriculum is beyond the scope of this chapter, but we provide several resources for differentiating high school content on the companion website.

Teach Students That Scientists in Particular Embrace Challenge and Hard Work, Learn From Mistakes, and Struggle With Problems

As we have discussed previously, in order for science to advance, people in the field must embrace challenge. Help students understand that challenge is part of the territory in science and that this is how discovery and advancement in the field happen (Hill, Corbett, & St. Rose, 2010). As you are making this point, be sure to remind students that mistakes are an important part of the learning process so that they don't interpret mistakes as automatic evidence that an activity is too difficult for them.

Communicate to Parents That Optimal Struggle Benefits Their Child

Help parents understand the same messages being communicated to the students. Just like their children, parents may also hold the belief that a challenging task signals a lack of ability. If parents understand that working hard on science homework is expected and does not mean their child is not cut out for science, they will be more likely to encourage their children to persist and seek help when they encounter a challenging task. Conversely, if parents observe that their children are doing their science homework quickly and easily, they can be powerful allies in communicating that perhaps their child requires more challenging work.

WHAT RESOURCES CAN SCIENCE TEACHERS USE TO PROMOTE POSITIVE CHALLENGE?

The companion website, http://www.niu.edu/eteams, contains useful resources to help teachers optimize challenge levels in their classrooms or that can be recommended for parents of their students. The following and more can be found on the website:

- Differentiation resources
- Practical guides for encouraging girls in science, technology, engineering, and math (STEM) subjects
- Links to related TED talks
- Streaming video clips of positive challenge in science class and of scientists talking about challenges they have overcome
- Further readings on optimal learning environments and engaging learning conditions

CHAPTER TEN

Emotion

Claire is very excited about her project in physical science class. Even though she hesitated to handle the worms at first, she has enjoyed composting—she brings garbage from her lunch every day to feed the worms and especially loves saving the worm cocoons when the class harvests compost. Ms. Behrer is thrilled by Claire's engagement in using the compost to grow food, her enthusiasm for conducting experiments with different soil mixes, and her excellent lab reports. She is very concerned about Claire's anxiety during testing, however. Claire does not seem able to show what she knows on tests.

WHAT EMOTIONS ARE LIKELY TO IMPACT MOTIVATION IN SCIENCE?

The term *emotion* describes an affective and physiological reaction to events. Emotions are usually temporary—people tend to experience many emotional fluctuations throughout any given day as they encounter different situations. Pekrun and his colleagues created a taxonomy of emotions that are typically experienced in academic settings (Pekrun, 1992; Pekrun, Frenzel, Goetz, & Perry, 2007). The emotions in this taxonomy can be categorized across several different dimensions. One of these dimensions, of course, is that emotions can be categorized as positive or negative affective states.

According to this taxonomy, positive affective states that are likely to occur in academic settings include enjoyment, relaxation, pride, and relief, among others. While emotions such as pride and relief tend to stem from one's performance in a class (Pekrun calls these *outcome-focused* positive emotions), enjoyment and relaxation tend to be derived from the learning activities themselves (*activity-focused* positive emotions). Within the activity-focused category of emotional responses, emotions can be seen as *activating* (as in the case of enjoyment) or *deactivating* (as is the case with relaxation). Pekrun's theory and related supporting research indicate that the positive activating emotions such as enjoyment tend to have the most positive effects on students achievement, as they increase motivation and improve flexible learning (Pekrun, Goetz, Frenzel, Barchfield, & Perry, 2011; Pekrun, Goetz, Titz, & Perry, 2002).

Negative emotions experienced by students in classrooms may include anger, anxiety, and sadness, among others (Pekrun et al., 2007). Fear is a basic and universal negative emotion that occurs in response to feeling threatened—individuals respond to perceptions of danger by either wanting to fight or flee (Mowrer, 1960). This reaction is widely associated with the term *stress*, and we will use that term, and the related term *anxiety*, throughout the remainder of the chapter. Many scholars who study emotions distinguish between *fear, stress,* and *anxiety*, but because our purpose here is to understand how stress and anxiety impact students in the classroom, the fine-grained differences delineated by scholars will have less relevance for us and so will not be described further. It is important to note that we are not addressing anxiety disorder, which should be diagnosed and monitored by a medical or psychological professional; rather, we are using the term as it refers to phenomena such as test anxiety, which has broad applications (recognizing that trait anxiety does exacerbate state anxiety).

Science anxiety has been identified as a unique form of anxiety through long-term research (Mallow, 2010). Wynstra and Cummings described different categories of science anxiety (1993, as cited in Britner's 2010 review of the science anxiety literature). Those categories are

- *danger anxiety*, pertaining to lab work or demonstrations involving fire or explosions;
- *squeamish anxiety*, involving some lab work (such as dissection or working with bodily fluids) or viewing specimens (preserved or caged animals such as spiders or snakes);

- *performance and classroom anxiety*, involving being observed or supervised;
- *test anxiety*, involving expectations of failure, being flooded with stress, and having difficulty retrieving knowledge; and
- *mathematics anxiety*, a distinct form of anxiety concerning math skills, which may come into play in science class.

WHY ARE STUDENT EMOTIONS IMPORTANT FOR HIGH SCHOOL SCIENCE TEACHERS TO CONSIDER?

Emotions Are Linked to Learning

Emotions influence learning through multiple pathways. Emotions change dopamine levels in the brain, which affect the way we process information and how we store and retrieve that information in long-term memory (Ashby, Isen, & Turken, 1999). Positive emotional experience enables us to better incorporate new information into our existing understanding and facilitates more generative, flexible, and creative processing of information (Fiedler, 2000; Pekrun et al., 2002). The stress response inhibits thinking and attention, thereby interfering with students' ability to learn content (Hinton & Fischer, 2010). Anxiety inhibits cognitive processing in terms of organizing, remembering (drawing a blank), and applying learned information in an academic setting (Stipek, 1998).

Emotions Are Linked to Motivation

Emotions impact an individual's drive to continue participating in an event or pursuing a goal. Positive emotions, such as enjoyment and joy, lead to intrinsic motivation for a task (Csikszentmihalyi, 1990; Linnenbrink & Pintrich, 2000). The link between positive emotions and task choice may extend well beyond the academic subjects students choose to engage in while in high school: Positive experience in particular subject areas in

Elena Elisseeva/Shutterstock

high school have been linked to students' future aspirations (Csikszentmihalyi & Schneider, 2000). The tendency to avoid those situations or experiences that provoke negative emotions is universal. Students are less likely to choose or persevere in pursuit of an interest or career if they are overwhelmed by stress or anxiety (Boekaerts, 2010); high school science students with science anxiety tend to have low science self-efficacy and choose not to persist in science (Britner, 2010).

Emotions Influence Performance

Emotions mediate the link between students' learning, goal orientation (see Chapter 7), and their achievement (Pekrun, Elliot, & Maier, 2009). A small amount of stress can aid performance by spurring on a student to invest extra time, effort, or attention into an activity, but excessive anxiety is debilitating and does not allow students to perform at their best (Stipek, 1998). The extensive empirical findings about this have strong implications in today's climate of high-stakes testing.

Emotion Is a Scientific Construct

Biology and anatomy teachers can link the physiological and cognitive aspects of emotion to basic concepts they teach, including evolution. Understanding the science behind emotions can be helpful for teachers and students and is clearly linked to basic content.

High School Students Are Sensitive to Emotion-Based Motivation

Adolescence is a period marked by heightened and fluctuating emotion. Anxiety in science tends to begin before high school and increases during the high school years (Britner, 2010). A majority of high school students—about 70 percent—report experiencing test anxiety (Cassady, 2010).

Teachers Can Influence Students' Emotions

Classroom practices have an impact on the emotions that students feel during class (Britner, 2010), so learning about this topic and related strategies could make teachers more effective and may ultimately have positive impacts on students.

WHAT HAVE RESEARCHERS DISCOVERED ABOUT STUDENT EMOTION IN SCIENCE CLASS?

Relative to other motivational constructs, the study of the role of emotions in learning is a new area, with a great deal of potential for future study. Research on emotions in science classrooms in particular has lagged behind other subject areas, and this is likely due in part to prevalent images of science as a discipline that tends to draw a sharp distinction between reason and feeling (Alsop & Watts, 2003). As is the case across all subject areas, the vast majority of research on emotion in science focuses on the negative emotion of anxiety. Much of the current work on positive emotions such as enjoyment in science is coming out of our own research group.

The Type of Class Activity Predicts Students' Emotions

In our Science-in-the-Moment (SciMo) project, students' responses about how they were feeling at the moment they were signaled varied depending on the particular science activity in which they were engaged. Figure 10.1 indicates how students felt when engaged in some of the most commonly observed science activities.

These patterns of emotion represent a paradox in that the learning activities that students saw as more enjoyable were relatively unimportant to them, and the less enjoyable activities were viewed as more important. For example, students reported the highest level of enjoyment in labs, but they also reported learning less in labs than during lecture and seatwork. They also reported that labs were the least important of any of the classroom activities they did. Students viewed tests as the most important classroom activity but—not surprisingly—reported low enjoyment and increased stress when testing. We imagine that the personal importance students placed on tests may reflect their desire to get good

Figure 10.1   How Students Feel in Various Science Activities

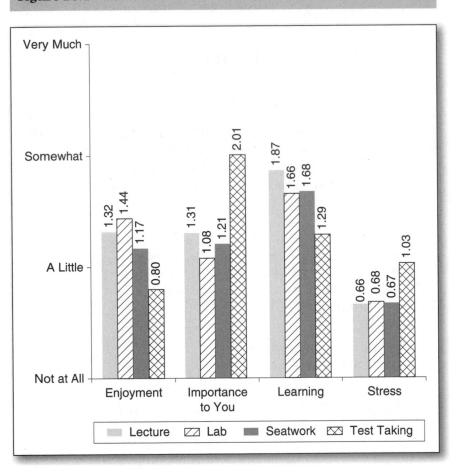

grades and a desire to achieve other goals that require good grades rather than a heightened sense of personal relevance of tests per se.

Test Anxiety Puts Students at a Disadvantage

There is an extensive body of research regarding student test anxiety (Cassady, 2010). Students who suffer from considerable test anxiety tend not to prepare well for tests (recall that a little anxiety can actually help students). Students with performance avoidance goals tend to procrastinate or use other self-handicapping strategies. Those with performance approach goals are likely to use surface study strategies (see Chapter 7). Interestingly, however, these highly anxious students actually spend more time studying than other students. The excessive studying does not help, because they tend to be outperformed by students who use more effective study and test-taking strategies (Cassady, 2010). The anxious students' disadvantage is further compounded by stress-related chemicals flooding the brain and interfering with memory function during the test. Students who are anxious about standardized tests in science tend to do poorly on all types of test questions (Britner, 2010). The ultimate result of anxiety and related underperformance in science is the student avoiding science-related activities and careers.

Emotions Vary by Subject Area

During high school, students' feelings about science vary between science subjects (Lau & Roeser, 2002). Students might enjoy one subject, such as biology, but dislike another, such as physics, or vice versa. Britner (2008) found that across different science subjects, high school students with performance avoidance goals were more anxious than students with mastery goals (see Chapter 7 for a discussion of goal orientation). Further, anxiety influenced students' confidence, self-esteem, and grades. Anxiety differed by gender and subject; these differences are explained in a subsequent section of the chapter.

Chepko Danil Vitalevich/Shutterstock

Regarding students' momentary reports of their emotions in science classes, we can use our own data to compare high school students' emotions in different science subjects. We found that students reported the highest levels of both enjoyment and stress in physics classrooms. Students reported the least enjoyment and the least stress in chemistry. Students reported that biology was relatively enjoyable (second only to physics) but not stressful (comparable to chemistry). Keep in mind that students also reported significantly lower levels of challenge in biology than in all other subject areas, where challenge levels were comparable to one another. It is notable that the general science class, where ninth graders were placed if they were reading below grade level, was generally characterized as unenjoyable, with high levels of stress.

Science Class Feels Different to Boys and Girls

Male students in the SciMo study reported having more pleasurable experiences in science classes than female students. Conversely, female students reported higher levels of stress than males during class (see Figure 10.2). These patterns were generally consistent across all science subjects. Note, however, that

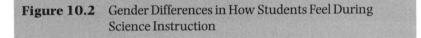

Figure 10.2   Gender Differences in How Students Feel During Science Instruction

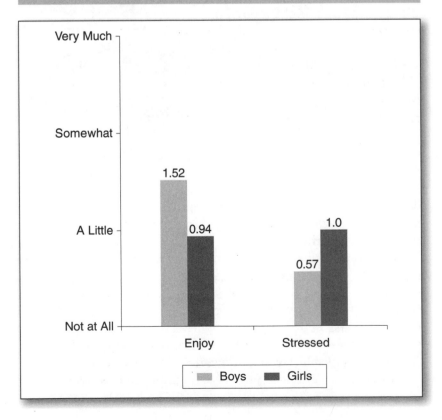

even though there were statistically significant gender differences, objectively speaking, both male and female students reported fairly low levels of enjoyment and stress in science.

Others have also found that female students have more anxiety in science class than males. For example, Mallow (2010) found that about two-thirds of the students he treated in his science anxiety clinic were female. Britner (2008) also found that female students had higher science anxiety in both biology and physical science, though she did not observe similar gender differences in earth science. Interestingly, anxiety appeared more detrimental to female students' performance and motivation in physical science than it was in biology, even though females' anxiety levels were higher than males' anxiety levels in that course, too.

Emotional Experience Is Related to Performance in Science

The small body of existing research that examines links between emotion and performance in science suggests that this is an area ripe for investigation. For example, Zusho, Pintrich, and Coppola (2003) found that the affective dimensions of students' classroom experiences were strong predictors of final course performance in college chemistry classes, even after controlling for prior achievement. We found similar results in our SciMo data. High school students who experienced stronger negative emotions in science had lower grades at the end of the school year relative to their peers, even after controlling for their grades prior to our study.

Science Anxiety Can Be Reduced

Mallow and his colleagues developed strategies to reduce science anxiety at a science anxiety clinic at Loyola University in Chicago (Mallow, 2006). The strategies were directed at helping students learn science more effectively, at reducing negative self-talk, and at teaching relaxation techniques. Extensive studies were carried out to test the approaches, which demonstrated that these strategies were effective relative to a control group (Mallow, 2006). A link to additional descriptions of these strategies can be found on our website.

Our research on the SciMo project indicates that creating positive emotional experiences for students in science may be a particularly effective strategy for reducing science anxiety among girls. We found that when boys were enjoying themselves and experiencing other positive emotions in science class, their anxiety about science decreased a little. For girls, however, there was a much bigger drop when they experienced positive emotions (Schmidt, Kackar, & Strati, 2010). Even though girls generally tend to be more anxious than boys about science, their anxiety may also be more easily soothed through the provision of positive emotional experience. While we do not mean to suggest that teachers' number-one objective should be to entertain their students, there is mounting empirical evidence that suggests that when students are enjoying themselves and feeling good in class, their anxiety is lower and they are able to focus their attention and learn more.

HOW CAN TEACHERS ENHANCE ENJOYMENT AND TEACH COPING SKILLS?

There are a number of ways that teachers can increase students' enjoyment and help them learn coping skills to manage anxiety. Those strategies are described here.

Choose Strategies for Increasing Enjoyment

There is no single prescription for increasing students' enjoyment in science class. Interest is one of many paths to enjoyment, so enjoyment can be enhanced by making the content more interesting to students either by creating novel learning activities (situational interest) or by connecting activities to students' existing individual interests (see Chapter 2). Students' enjoyment will also be heightened by promoting a positive and nonthreatening classroom environment (see Chapter 3) or by providing challenging activities that invite students to engage deeply in their learning activities (see Chapter 9). Another option for increasing student enjoyment that has not been discussed in other chapters of this book is humor. Teachers' use of humor in the classroom has been shown to increase students' positive emotions as well as decreasing negative ones (Bennett, 2003; Garner, 2006; Stambor, 2006). A study of physics classrooms from our research group (Zaleski & Lyutykh, 2012) suggests that teachers who use more humor, even about unrelated content material, have students who enjoy physics more and are more engaged in content-related activities.

Target the Source of Anxiety

As with many educational interventions, anxiety reduction is most beneficial if it is targeted at the source of the problem—there is no one-size-fits-all solution (Britner, 2010; Cassady, 2010). For example, students with good study habits but extreme evaluative anxiety will benefit from relaxation techniques but do not need extra help on study skills. Students who hold performance goals benefit from having their beliefs and study skills challenged in the learning and test reflection phases (Cassady, 2010).

Wavebreakmedia Shutterstock

Teachers also can be sensitive to the types of science anxiety that students experience and plan accordingly to emphasize safety precautions in the case of danger anxiety and to allow desensitization in the case of squeamish anxiety by allowing students to look at pictures and models, do virtual dissection, or observe live specimens from a distance that feels safe to them. Stipek (1998) also emphasizes the importance of recognizing that anxiety-reducing measures are often not necessary for students who do not experience excessive anxiety and could actually inhibit the benefits to be derived from minor stress.

Encourage Positive Self-Talk

An effective technique for coping with stress and reducing anxiety is positive self-talk (Seligman, 2004). Students can be taught to use this technique very quickly and easily. Essentially, students can be told that positive self-talk involves focusing on the present, telling oneself the steps to take in the here and now, giving oneself encouragement, and turning negative thoughts around. Practicing the technique can be done by pairing students and having one read a negative statement such as "I'm going to fail" or "I can't get this" and having the other student turn the statement into a positive one such as "I know I can pass this if I study" or "I can learn this with some effort." Teachers will greatly enhance the internalization of this skill by identifying student use of negative self-talk and reminding them to use positive self-talk.

Teach Study Skills and Reduce Cognitive Load

Students who have generalized test anxiety and poor study skills can benefit from learning general study skills within the context of their course material (see Chapter 7). Those students whose anxiety is exclusive to science might benefit from specialized focus on study skills that are especially important for science (Mallow, 1991). Visualization and interpretation of visual displays (e.g., models, graphs) are essential for science learning. Reading a science textbook, writing a lab report or even science notes, and solving scientific problems require specialized scientific literacy skills that can be acquired if they are taught but are unlikely to be generalized from those literacy skills typically taught in English class.

Encourage Effective Test-Taking Strategies

Anxious students can be taught to do things such as underline key words in questions to focus their attention or to look for and answer the questions about which they are most confident first. The Educational Testing Service (ETS) provides a student guide for reducing test anxiety, and American College Testing (ACT) provides a guide for science test-taking strategies. Those resources are linked to the companion website.

Teach Relaxation Response

There are several efficient methods for teaching students to relax when they are tense. One way is through deep breathing techniques. Another is through progressive relaxation techniques. Mindfulness is yet another approach (Inzlicht, Tullett, Legault, & Kang, 2011). Some teachers spend several minutes before a test having students who want to participate in mindfulness exercises do so while other students simply sit quietly. Others can provide these resources to students for them to learn on their own. Yet others ask guidance counselors to teach and/or lead students in these techniques. Refer to Chapter 8 and our companion website for more information on mindfulness and other relaxation techniques.

WHAT RESOURCES CAN SCIENCE TEACHERS USE TO PROMOTE ENJOYMENT AND DECREASE ANXIETY?

The companion website, http://www.niu.edu/eteams, contains resources that can help teachers increase enjoyment and decrease anxiety in their science classroom or that can be recommended for parents of their students. The following and more can be found on the website:

- Links to emotion motivation questionnaires
- Links to websites with instructions for relaxation, breathing, and mindfulness techniques
- Links to websites with anxiety intervention tips and test-taking strategies
- Study skills resources
- Additional readings on science anxiety
- Streaming video clips demonstrating the practices discussed in this chapter

Appendix

METHODOLOGY OF THE SciMo STUDY

Context of the Study

The Science-in-the-Moment (SciMo) study took place over the course of one school year in a single comprehensive high school serving students from a diverse community located on the fringe of a large metropolitan area. The school serves 9th–12th graders, with an enrollment of approximately 3,300 in 2009. Forty percent of the student body was White, 38 percent Hispanic, 19 percent African American, and 3 percent Asian. Thirty-three percent of students in the school were considered *low income*. The graduation rate was 74 percent. Average class size was 23.6 students.

Participants in the Study

Data were collected from students and teachers in 12 regular-track science classrooms, three classrooms each in the areas of general science, biology, chemistry, and physics.

Teachers

Thirteen teachers in 12 classrooms participated in the study (a new teacher was assigned to one of the general science classes in the spring semester as a result of staffing changes elsewhere in the department). Six of the teachers were male and seven were female. It is noteworthy that all of the biology teachers were female and all of the physics teachers were male, while the general science and chemistry classrooms that were studied had both male and female teachers. As is the case in the science department

as a whole, all participant teachers were White. The teachers in
the study had an average of 8.6 years of teaching experience, and
the average age was 35.6. Three teacher participants (one biology,
one chemistry, and one physics) had earned National Board
Certification. The science department chairperson reported that
the inquiry approach to science instruction had been adopted and
was used by all science teachers in the school.

Students

In total, 244 students participated in the study. The overall
student participation rate across all classrooms was 91 percent;
half of the classrooms that were studied had 100 percent participation. The student sample was 53 percent male and 47 percent
female. According to school records, 43 percent of students in the
sample were eligible to receive free or reduced lunch.

Table A.1   Participants in the SciMo Study

Student Participants	% of Sample	Teacher Participants	# of Teachers
Sex		**Sex**	
Male	53	Male	6
Female	47	Female	7
Race		**Race**	
Hispanic	42	White	13
White	37	**National Board Certification**	3
Black	12	**Education Level Completed**	
Multiracial	6	Four-Year College Degree	5
Asian/Pacific Islander	2	Master's Degree	7
American Indian	1	PhD or Other Advanced Degree	1

Student Participants	% of Sample		Teacher Participants	# of Teachers
Subject				**# of Years**
General Science	20			
Biology	32		**Mean Age**	35.6
Chemistry	23		**Mean Years of Teaching Experience (Range 2–19)**	8.6
Physics	25			
Grade Level				
9th	43			
10th	21			
11th	34			
12th	2			
Free/Reduced Lunch	43			
Parent Education				
High School or Less	34			
Some College	16			
Graduated from College	19			
Advanced Degree	14			
Don't Know	17			

The students in our sample had high educational expectations for themselves (see Figure A.1). Seventy-one percent of the students in our sample expect to complete a college education or pursue an advanced degree. It is notable that more than 10 percent of the students we surveyed did not have clear educational expectations for themselves.

Figure A.1   Students' Educational Expectations

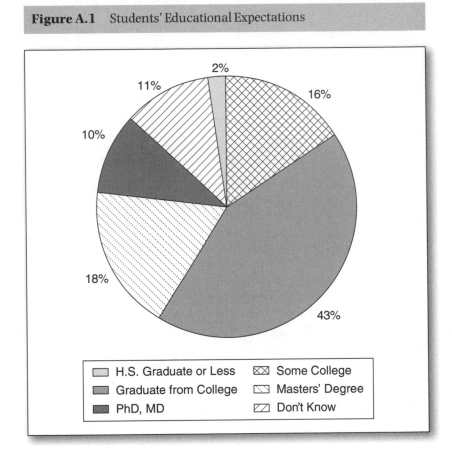

Data Collection

How Data Were Collected

Methods of data collection included traditional surveys, experience sampling techniques, videotaping, classroom observation, and teacher interviews. Each teacher was interviewed about one of the observed instructional units. Course grades, cumulative GPA, and free/reduced lunch status were collected from school records.

Teacher Surveys

During the fall data collection wave, participant teachers completed a survey in which they provided information about their demographic characteristics, professional training, and current teaching assignment. Also included in this survey was the Problems in Schools Questionnaire (PIS; Deci, Schwartz, Sheinman, & Ryan, 1981; Reeve, Bolt, & Cai, 1999), which provided a measure of teacher autonomy support.

Student Surveys

In both the fall and spring data collection waves, students completed a survey. The fall survey focused on students' demographic characteristics, educational and occupational aspirations, and school experiences. The survey included a measure of perceptions of teacher autonomy support from The Learning Climate Questionnaire (LCQ; Black & Deci, 2000; Williams & Deci, 1996) and a measure of perceived competence from the Perceived Competence for Learning Scale (Williams & Deci, 1996). The spring survey focused on the kinds of educational supports and resources available in students' homes. Both the fall and spring surveys included Gogolin and Swartz's (1992) Attitudes toward Science Inventory.

Experience Sampling Method

During each wave of data collection, students' subjective experience in each science classroom was measured repeatedly over a period of five consecutive school days using a variant of the Experience Sampling Method (ESM; Csikszentmihalyi & Larson, 1987). Participants wore a vibrating pager that was used to signal them unobtrusively using a remote transmitter at two randomly selected time points during each day's science class. To minimize the disruption to class flow and maximize the variety of classroom activities recorded, the pool of participants in each classroom was divided in half, with each half following a different signal schedule. In response to each signal, students completed an Experience Sampling Form (ESF) in which they briefly recorded their activities and thoughts at the time of the signal as well as various dimensions of their subjective experience. The ESF took approximately 1–2 minutes to complete. In an open-ended format, students provided brief descriptions of their thoughts and activities at the time of the signal. Responses were coded by trained coders using detailed coding schemes. Inter-rater reliability on these items was high, with percent agreement between two independent coders at 91.8 percent for primary activity, 89.3 percent for secondary activity, and 90 percent for thoughts.

Using Likert-type scales, students reported on multiple dimensions of their subjective experience. By the completion of the study, each participant had reported on multiple aspects of subjective experience on as many as 20 separate occasions, with each descriptive array linked to a specific course, content unit, and classroom activity. In total, 4,136 such responses were collected. In the fall semester, 2,139 responses were collected for an average of 9.2 responses per participant (92 percent signal response rate). In the spring semester, 1,997 responses were collected for an average of 9.1 responses per participant (91 percent signal response rate). Participant nonresponse to the ESM was nearly entirely attributable to school absence.

The method has a high degree of external or ecological validity, capturing participants' responses in everyday life. There are indications that the internal validity of the ESM is stronger than one-time questionnaires as well. Zuzanek (1999) has shown that the immediacy of the questions reduces the potential for failure of recall and the tendency to choose responses on the basis of social desirability (see Csikszentmihalyi & Larson, 1987, and Hektner, Schmidt, & Csikszentmihalyi, 2007, for a review).

Classroom Observations

During the five days of ESM signaling in both fall and spring, a trained observer was present to rate several dimensions of the teachers' and students' behavior. At the end of each lesson, the observers completed a brief global rating scale characterizing the nature of the class session they just observed. Using 5-point Likert-type scales, observers rated the class session in terms of the general level of challenge the lesson appeared to pose to students, students' skill level and engagement in class, and teacher autonomy support of and interaction with students. Observers rated whether certain behaviors were equally distributed between male and female students (M=F) or occurred more frequently with one gender (M>F or F>M), including (a) teacher engagement of students, (b) student participation in class, (c) teacher behavior management, (d) student cooperation, (e) teacher messages of competence, and (f) student display of competence/confidence. Inter-rater reliabilities were conducted for 25 percent of the observations; inter-rater reliabilities as indicated by percent agreement were adequate (above 80 percent).

At the end of each lesson, an observer also asked the teacher to indicate how typical that day's class was on a scale of 1–5 (with 5 being very typical). On the whole, teachers indicated that the lessons observed were rather typical, with an average rating of 3.9. Of the 120 lessons observed, 86 (71.6 percent) were rated by teachers as "somewhat" or "very" typical (ratings of 4 or 5), and only 2 lessons (or 1.7 percent) were rated as "not at all typical" (a rating of 1).

During the five days of ESM signaling in both fall and spring, a videographer with a camera and an additional trained observer were positioned in all classrooms to unobtrusively record classroom activities. The focus of the video was on the teacher's activities. The video footage was marked to indicate exactly when all ESM signals were emitted so that the instructional practices preceding students' subjective ratings could be coded and examined in relation to their activities. In both spring and fall, additional data were collected through traditional surveys, classroom observational ratings, and teacher interviews.

When Data Were Collected

Within each of the 12 classrooms, data were collected at two time points during the academic year—once each in fall and in spring. ESM and observational data were collected during one week in fall and one week in spring. Surveys were collected before the classroom data. Interviews with teachers were held after one of the weeks of data collection. Data from school records were collected after the end of the school year.

Data from different sections of the same course were collected during the same time period so that the data collected from all three sections would represent the same point in the science curriculum, thus enabling analysis of the effects of particular content units while controlling for the effects of the instructor. Studying two different content units from each course reduces the possibility that findings regarding a particular course were idiosyncratic and entirely attributable to the specific unit examined.

Data Coding

Instructional Practice Video Coding

Videos were coded twice. In the first round of coding, we coded all 100 hours of video for instructional practices. The eight general practices we identified were lecture, seatwork, testing, labs, discussion, movies, noninstructional time (e.g., classroom management), and off-task activity. Figure 1.1 in Chapter 1 illustrates how often each of these practices was observed.

Teachers' Verbal Interaction Video Coding

In the second round of coding, we completed a more detailed coding of teachers' verbal interactions with their students. We coded each teacher utterance on five different dimensions. A teacher's statement was considered a single utterance so long as it had a consistency in the person being addressed and the function of the statement. Therefore, utterances could be very short (e.g., "Everyone take out your homework") or much longer (e.g., a two-minute mini-lecture on the differences between exothermic and endothermic reactions). The 50-minute class sessions observed in this study typically contained 250–400 teacher utterances.

The five dimensions on which each utterance was coded are as follows: (1) who was addressed by the utterance (e.g., whole class, individual male, individual female, male small group, female small group, mixed small group); (2) who initiated the utterance (teacher or student); (3) whether or not the utterance was a question; (4) whether or not the utterance fostered student thinking; and (5) the function or purpose of the utterance. Following procedures previously used by King, Shumow, and Lietz (2001), the function of each utterance was categorized as (a) *content* (presenting declaratory science content knowledge), (b) *sequential flow* (moving the lesson forward by focusing on what has to happen next), (c) *elaboration* (focus on explanation, conceptual understanding, meaning making), (d) *classroom management*; or (e) *irrelevant to science* (chatting, general school announcements).

The SciMo Project was supported by the National Science Foundation under Grant No: HRD-0827526. Any opinions, findings, conclusions, or recommendations expressed in this material are those of the author(s) and do not reflect the views of the National Science Foundation.

References

Acar, B., & Tarhan, L. (2007). Effect of cooperative learning strategies on students' understanding of concepts in electrochemistry. *International Journal of Science and Mathematics Education, 5*(2), 349–373.

Acar, B., & Tarhan, L. (2008). Effects of cooperative learning on students' understanding of metallic bonding. *Research in Science Education, 38*(4), 401–420.

Allen, J., Gregory, A., Mikami, A., Lun, J., Hamre, B., & Pianta, R. (2012). *Predicting adolescent achievement with the CLASS-S Observation tool.* Retrieved from http://curry.virginia.edu/uploads/resourceLibrary/Research_brief_CLASS-S4.pdf

Alsop, S., & Watts, M. (2003). Science education and affect. *International Journal of Science Education, 25*(9), 1043–1047.

Ames, C. (1992). Achievement goals and the classroom motivational climate. In D. H. Schunk & J. Meece (Eds.), *Student perceptions in the classroom* (pp. 327–348). Hillsdale, NJ: Erlbaum.

Ames, C., Khoju, M., & Watkins, T. (1993). *Parent involvement: The relationship between school-to-home communication and parents' perceptions and beliefs* (Report No. 15). Urbana, IL: ERIC Document Service No. ED362271, Center on Families, Communities, Schools, and Children's Learning, University of Illinois.

Anderman, E., & Anderman, L. (2010). *Classroom motivation.* Upper Saddle River, NJ: Pearson.

Anderman, E, Austin, C. C., & Johnson, D. (2002). The development of goal orientation. In A. Wigfield & J. Eccles (Eds.), *Development of achievement motivation* (pp. 197–220). San Francisco, CA: Academic Press.

Anderman, E., & Sinatra, G. (2009). *The challenges of teaching and learning about science in the 21st century: Exploring the abilities and constraints of adolescent learners.* Paper commissioned by the National Academy of Education. Retrieved from http://www7.nationalacademies.org/bose/Anderson_Sinatra_Paper.pdf

Anderman, E., & Wolters, C. (2006). Goals, values and affect. In P. Alexander & P. Winne (Eds.), *Handbook of educational psychology* (pp. 369–390). Mahwah, NJ: Erlbaum.

Anderman, E., & Young, A. (1994). Motivation and strategy use in science: Individual differences and classroom effects. *Journal of Research in Science Teaching, 38*(1), 811–831.

Anderman, L., Andrzejewski, C., & Allen, J. (2011). How do teachers support students' motivation and learning in their classrooms? *Teachers College Record, 113*(5), 969–1003.

Andre, T., Whigham, M., Hendrickson, A., & Chambers, S. (1999). Competency beliefs, positive affect, and gender stereotypes of elementary students and their parents about science versus other school subjects. *Journal of Research in Science Teaching, 36*(6), 719–747.

Aronson, J., & Good, C. (2003). The development and consequences of stereotype vulnerability in adolescents. In F. Pajares & T. Urdan (Eds.), *Adolescence and education: Vol. 2, Academic motivation of adolescents* (pp. 299–330). Greenwich, CT: Information Age Publishing.

Aronson, J., Quinn, D., & Spencer, S. (1998). Stereotype threat and the academic performance of minorities and women. In J. Swim & C. Stangor (Eds.), *Prejudice: The target's perspective* (pp. 83–103). San Diego, CA: Academic Press.

Aschbacher, P. R., Li, E., & Roth, E. J. (2010). Is science me? High school students' identities, participation and aspirations in science, engineering, and medicine. *Journal of Research in Science Teaching, 47*(5), 564–582.

Ashby, F. G., Isen, A. M., & Turken, A. U. (1999). A neuropsychological theory of positive affect and its influence on cognition. *Psychological Review, 106*(3), 529–550.

Assor, A., Kaplan, H., & Roth, G. (2002). Choice is good, but relevance is excellent. *British Journal of Educational Psychology, 72,* 261–278.

Baird, J. R., & Penna, C. (1997). Perceptions of challenge in science learning. *International Journal of Science Education, 19*(10), 1195–1209.

Baker, D., & Leary, R. (1995). Letting girls speak out about science. *Journal of Research in Science Teaching, 32*(1), 3–27.

Bandura, A. (1986). *Social foundations of thought and action: A social cognitive theory.* Englewood Cliffs, NF: Prentice-Hall.

Bandura, A. (1997). *Self-efficacy: The exercise of control.* New York, NY: Freeman.

Barmby, P., Kind, P. M., & Jones, K. (2008). Examining changing attitudes in secondary school science. *International Journal of Science Education, 30*(8), 1075–1093.

Barron, K. E., & Harackiewicz, J. M. (2001). Achievement goals and optimal motivation: Testing multiple goal models. *Journal of Personality and Social Psychology, 80*(5), 706–722.

Beilock, S. L., Gunderson, E. A., Ramirez, G., & Levine, S. C. (2010). Female teachers' math anxiety affects girls' math achievement. *Proceedings of the National Academy of Sciences, 107*(5), 1860–1863.

Bennett, H. J. (2003). Humor in medicine. *Southern Medical Journal, 96*(12), 1257–1261.

Benware, C., & Deci, E. L. (1984). The quality of learning with an active versus passive motivational set. *American Educational Research Journal, 21*(4), 755–766.

Black, A. E., & Deci, E. L. (2000). The effects of instructors' autonomy support and students' autonomous motivation on learning organic chemistry: A self-determination theory perspective. *Science Education, 84*(6), 740–756.

Blackwell, L. S., Trzesniewski, K., & Dweck, C. S. (2007). Implicit theories of intelligence predict achievement across an adolescent transition: A longitudinal study and an intervention. *Child Development, 78*(1), 246–263.

Boekaerts, M. (2010). The crucial role of emotion and motivation in classroom learning. In B. Francisco, I. David, & D. Hanna (Eds.), *The nature of learning: Using research to inspire practices.* (pp. 91–111). OECD Publishing. Retrieved from http://www.oecd.org/edu/ceri/thenatureoflearningusingresearchtoinspirepractice.htm

Boutte, G., Kelly-Jackson, C., & Johnson, G. (2010). Culturally relevant teaching in science classrooms: Addressing academic achievement, cultural competence, and critical consciousness. *International Journal of Multicultural Education, 12*(2). Retrieved from http://ijme-journal.org/index.php/ijme/article/view/343/512

Brickhouse, N. W., Lowery, P., & Schultz, K. (2000). What kind of a girl does science? The construction of school science identities. *Journal of Research in Science Teaching, 37*(5), 441–458.

Britner, S. L. (2008). Motivation in high school science students: A comparison of gender differences in life, physical, and earth science classes. *Journal of Research in Science Teaching, 45*(8), 955–970.

Britner, S. L. (2010). Science anxiety: Relationships to achievement, self-efficacy and pedagogical factors. In J. Cassady (Ed.), *Anxiety in schools: The causes, consequences, and solutions for academic anxieties* (pp. 80–95). New York, NY: Peter Lang.

Burnett, C. P. (2002). Teacher praise and feedback and students' perceptions of the classroom environment. *Educational Psychology, 22*(1), 5–16.

Carlone, H. (2004). The cultural production of science in reform-based physics: Girls' access, participation, and resistance. *Journal of Research in Science Teaching, 41*(4), 392–414.

Cassady, J. (2010). Test anxiety: Contemporary theories and implications for learning. In J. Cassady (Ed.), *Anxiety in schools: The causes, consequences, and solutions for academic anxieties* (pp. 5–26). New York, NY: Peter Lang.

Catsambis, S. (1995). Gender, race, ethnicity and science education in the middle grades. *Journal of Research in Science Teaching, 32*(3), 242–257.

Chirkov, V. I., & Ryan, R. M. (2001). Parent and teacher autonomy-support in Russian and U.S. adolescents: Common effects on well-being and academic motivation. *Journal of Cross Cultural Psychology, 32*(5), 618–635.

Csikszentmihalyi, M. (1990). *Flow: The psychology of optimal experience.* New York, NY: Harper & Row.

Csikszentmihalyi, M. (1997). *Finding flow: The psychology of engagement with everyday life.* New York, NY: Basic.

Csikszentmihalyi, M., & Larson, R. (1987). Validity and reliability of the Experience Sampling Method. *Journal of Nervous and Mental Disease, 175*(9), 526–536.

Csikszentmihalyi, M., & Schneider, B. (2000). *Becoming adult: How teenagers prepare for the world of work.* New York, NY: Basic.

Dall'Alba, G., & Sandberg, J. (2006). Unveiling professional development. *Review of Educational Research, 76*(3), 383–412.

Daniels, D., & Shumow, L. (2003). Child development and classroom teaching: A review of the literature and implications for educating teachers. *Journal of Applied Developmental Psychology, 23*(5), 495–526.

Daniels, H. (2011). Vygotsky and psychology. In U. Goswami (Ed.), *Handbook of childhood cognitive development* (2nd ed., pp. 673–696). New York, NY: Wiley Blackwell.

Darby-Hobbs, L. (2011). Responding to a relevance imperative in school science and mathematics: Humanising the curriculum through story. *Research in Science Education.* Retrieved from http://deakin .academia.edu/LindaHobbs/Papers/892945/Responding_to_a_relevance_imperative_in_school_science_and_mathematics_Humanising_the_curriculum_through_story

Davis, E., Petish, D., & Smithey, J. (2006). Challenges new science teachers face. *Review of Educational Research, 76*(4), 607–651.

Deci, E. L. (1975). *Intrinsic motivation.* New York, NY: Plenum Press.

Deci, E. L., Koestner, R., Ryan, R. M. (1999). A meta-analytic review of experiments examining the effects of extrinsic rewards on intrinsic motivation. *Psychological Bulletin, 125*(6), 627–668.

Deci, E. L., Koestner, R., & Ryan, R. M. (2001). Extrinsic rewards and intrinsic motivation in education: Reconsidered once again. *Review of Educational Research, 71*(1), 1–27.

Deci, E. L., & Ryan, R. M. (1985). *Intrinsic motivation and self-determination in human behavior.* New York, NY: Plenum.

Deci, E. L., & Ryan, R. M. (1991). A motivational approach to self: Integration in personality. In R. A. Dienstbier (Ed.), *Nebraska symposium on motivation 1990* (vol. 38, pp. 237–288). Lincoln: University of Nebraska Press.

Deci, E. L., Schwartz, A. J., Sheinman, L., & Ryan, R. M. (1981). An instrument to assess adults' orientations toward control versus autonomy with children: Reflections on intrinsic motivation and perceived competence. *Journal of Educational Psychology, 73*(5), 642–650.

Dornbusch, S. M., & Kaufman, J. G. (2001). The social structure of the American high school. In T. Urdan & F. Pajares (Eds.), *Adolescence and education: General issues in the education of adolescents* (pp. 61–93). Greenwich, CT: Information Age Publishing.

Dweck, C. S. (1999). *Self-theories: Their role in motivation, personality, and development.* Philadelphia, PA: Psychology Press.

Dweck, C. S. (2002). Messages that motivate: How praise molds students' beliefs, motivation and performance in surprising ways. In J. Aronson (Ed.), *Improving academic achievement: Impact of psychological factors on education* (pp. 38–61). San Diego, CA: Academic Press.

Dweck, C. S. (2006a). Is math a gift? Beliefs that put females at risk. In S. Ceci & W. Williams (Eds.), *Why aren't more women in science? Top researchers debate the evidence* (pp. 47–55). Washington, DC: American Psychological Association.

Dweck, C. S. (2006b). *Mindset: The new psychology of success.* New York, NY. Random House.

Dweck, C. S. (2007). The perils and promise of praise. *Educational Leadership, 65*(2), 34–39. Retrieved from http://www.ascd.org/publica tions/educational-leadership/oct07/vol65/num02/The-Perils-and-Promises-of-Praise.aspx

Dweck, C. S., & Leggett, E. L. (1988). A social-cognitive approach to motivation and personality. *Psychological Review, 95*(2), 256–273.

Eccles, J. S. (1983). Expectancies, values and academic behaviors. In J. T. Spence (Ed.), *Achievement and achievement motives* (pp. 75–146). San Francisco, CA: Freeman.

Eccles, J. S., Adler, T. F., Futterman, R., Goff, S. B., Kaczala, C. M., Meece, J. L., & Midgley, C. (1983). Expectancies, values, and academic behaviors. In J. T. Spence (Ed.), *Achievement and achievement motivation* (pp. 75–146). San Francisco, CA: W. H. Freeman.

Eccles, J. S., Midgley, C., Wigfield, A., Miller-Buchanan, C., Reuman, D., Flanagan, C., & MacIver, D. (1993). Development during adolescence: The impact of stage-environment fit on young adolescents' experience in schools and families. *American Psychologist, 48*(2), 90–101.

Elliot, A. J. (1997). Integrating the "classic" and "contemporary" approaches to achievement motivation: A hierarchical model of approach and avoidance achievement motivation. In M. Maehr & P. Pintrich (Eds.), *Advances in motivation and achievement* (vol. 10, pp. 243–279). Greenwich, CT: JAI Press.

Elliott, E. S., & Dweck, C. S. (1988). Goals: An approach to motivation and achievement. *Journal of Personality and Social Psychology, 54*(1), 5–12.

Farmer, T. W., McAuliffe Lines, M., & Hamm, J. V. (2011). Revealing the invisible hand: The role of teachers in children's's peer experiences. *Journal of Applied Developmental Psychology, 32*(5), 247–256.

Fiedler, K. (2000). Toward an integrative account of affect and cognition phenomena using the BIAS computer algorithm. In J. Forgas (Ed.), *Feeling and thinking: The role of affect in social cognition* (pp. 223–252). New York, NY: Cambridge University Press.

Frome, P., & Eccles, J. (1998). Parents' influence on children's achievement-related perceptions. *Journal of Personality and Social Psychology, 74*(2), 435–452.

Garner, R. L. (2006). Humor in pedagogy: How ha-ha can lead to aha! *College Teaching, 54*(1), 177–180.

Gentry, M., Rizza, M. G., & Owen, S. V. (2002). Examining perceptions of challenge and choice in classrooms: The relationship between teachers and their students and comparisons between gifted students and other students. *Gifted Child Quarterly, 46*(2), 145–155.

George, R. (2000). Measuring change in students' attitudes toward science over time: An application of latent variable growth modeling. *Journal of Science Education and Technology, 9*(3), 213–225.

Gogolin, L., & Swartz, F. (1992). A quantitative and qualitative inquiry into the attitudes toward science of nonscience college students. *Journal of Research in Science Teaching, 29*(5), 487–504.

Gonzalez, A., Doan Holbein, M., & Quilter, S. (2002). High school students' goal orientations and their relationship to perceived parenting styles. *Contemporary Educational Psychology, 27*(3), 450–470.

Good, M., Aronson, J., & Inzlicht, M. (2003). Improving adolescents' standardized test performance: An intervention to reduce the effects of stereotype threat. *Applied Developmental Psychology, 24*(6), 645–662.

Goodenow, C. (1993). The psychological sense of school membership among adolescents: Scale development and educational correlates. *Psychology in the Schools, 30*(1), 79–91.

Gottfried, A., Fleming, J., & Gottfried, A. (2001). Continuity of academic intrinsic motivation from childhood through late adolescence: A longitudinal study. *Journal of Educational Psychology, 93*(1), 3–13.

Grant, H., & Dweck, C. S. (2003). Clarifying achievement goals and their impact. *Journal of Personality and Social Psychology, 85*(3), 541–553.

Greenfield, T. (1996). Gender, ethnicity, science achievement and attitudes. *Journal of Research in Science Teaching, 33*(8), 259–275.

Grolnick, W. S., Ryan, R. M., & Deci, E. L. (1991). The inner resources for school achievement: Motivational mediators of children's perceptions of their parents. *Journal of Educational Psychology, 83*(4), 508–517.

Halpern, D., Aronson, J., Reimer, N., Simpkins, S., Star, J., & Wentzel, K. (2007). *Encouraging girls in math and science* (NCER Report No. 2007–2003). Washington, DC: National Center for Education Research, Institute of Education Sciences, U.S. Department of Education.

Harackiewicz, J. (2010, March). *Optimal motivation in education: The interface of achievement goal, interest, and expectancy-value theories.* Keynote address, Northern Illinois University Graduate Student Research Conference, DeKalb, IL.

Hardre, P., & Sullivan, D. (2009). Motivating adolescents: High school teachers' perceptions and classroom practices. *Teacher Development, 13*(1), 1–16.

Harter, S. (2009). Effectance motivation reconsidered: Toward a developmental model. *Human Development, 21*(1), 34–64.

Hazari, Z., Potvin, G., Tai, R., & Almarode, J. (2010). For the love of learning science: Connecting learning orientation and career productivity in physics and chemistry. *Physics Education Research, 6,* 010107-1-010107-9.

Hazari, Z., Tai, R., & Sadler, P. (2007). Gender differences in introductory university physics performance: The influence of high school physics preparation and affective factors. *Science Education, 91*(6), 847–876.

Hektner, J. M., Schmidt, J. A., & Csikszentmihalyi, M. (2007). *Experience sampling method: Measuring the quality of everyday life.* Thousand Oaks, CA: SAGE.

Hidi, S. (2006). Interest: A unique motivational variable. *Educational Research Review, 1*(2), 69–82.

Hidi, S., & Renninger, K. (2006). The four-phase model of interest development. *Educational Psychologist, 41*(2), 111–127.

Hill, C., Corbett, C., & St. Rose, E. (2010). *Why so few? Women in science, technology, engineering and mathematics.* Washington, DC: American Association of University Women.

Hinton, C., & Fischer, K. (2010). Learning from the developmental and biological perspective. In B. Francisco, I. David, & D. Hanna (Eds.), *The nature of learning: Using research to inspire practices* (pp. 113–133).

OECD Publishing. Retrieved from http://www.oecd.org/edu/ceri/thenatureoflearningusingresearchtoinspirepractice.htm

Hofer, M. (2010). Adolescents' development of individual interests: A product of multiple goal regulation? *Educational Psychologist, 45*(3), 149–166.

Holmes, N. (2002). *The two mindsets.* San Carlos, CA: Mindset Works Inc.

Hulleman, C., & Harackiewicz, J. (2009). Promoting interest and performance in high school science classes. *Science, 326*(5958), 1410–1412.

Inzlicht, M., Tullett, A., Legault, L., & Kang, S. (2011). Lingering effects: Stereotype threat hurts more than you think. *Social Issues and Policy Review, 5*(1), 227–256. Retrieved from http://www.michaelinzlicht.com/wp/wp-content/uploads/downloads/2011/12/Inzlicht-Tullett-Legault-Kang-2011.pdf

James, H. M. (2002). *Why do girls persist in science? A qualitative study of the decision-making processes of pre-adolescent and adolescent girls* (Unpublished doctoral dissertation). Harvard University, Cambridge, MA.

Johnson, D. W., & Johnson, R. T. (1987). *Learning together and alone: Cooperative, competitive, and individualistic learning.* Englewood Cliffs, NJ: Prentice-Hall.

Kalkman, D. L., & DeFrates-Densch, N. (2011, April). *Student engagement and autonomy during high school science instruction.* Paper presented at the annual meeting of the American Educational Research Association, New Orleans, LA.

Kalkman, D. L., DeFrates-Densch, N., Smith, M C., & Ochoa-Angrino, S. (2010, May). *Do high school students' experiences and perceptions of autonomy support during science instruction predict changes in their attitudes toward science?* Paper presented at the annual meeting of the American Educational Research Association, Denver, CO.

Kaplan, A., & Maehr, M. (2007). The contribution and prospects of goal orientation theory. *Educational Psychology Review, 19*, 141–187.

Katz, I., & Assor, A. (2007). When choice motivates and when it does not. *Educational Psychology Review, 19*(2), 429–442.

King, K., Shumow, L., & Lietz, S. (2001). Science education in an urban elementary school: Case studies of teacher beliefs and classroom practices. *Science Education, 85*(2), 89–110.

Klem, A. M., & Connell, J. P. (2004). Relationships matter: Linking teacher support to student engagement and achievement. *Journal of School Health, 74*(7), 262–273.

Koballa, T. R, & Glynn, S. M. (2007). Attitudinal and motivational constructs in science learning. In S. K. Abell & N. G. Lederman (Eds.), *Handbook of research on science education* (pp. 75–102). New York, NY: Psychology Press.

Kunter, M., Frenzel, A., Nagy, G., Baumert, J., & Pekrun, R. (2011). Teacher enthusiasm: Dimensionality and context specificity. *Contemporary Educational Psychology, 36*(4), 289–301.

Lau, S., & Roeser, R. W. (2002). Cognitive abilities and motivational processes in high school students' situational engagement and achievement in science. *Educational Assessment, 8*(2), 139–162.

Lee, V., & Berkham, D. (1996). Gender differences in middle grade science achievement: Subject-domain, ability level and course emphasis. *Science Education, 80*(6), 613–650.

Lent, R. W., Brown, S. D., Gover, M. R., & Nijjer, S. K. (1996). Cognitive assessment of the sources of mathematics self-efficacy: A thought-listing analysis. *Journal of Career Assessment, 4*(1), 33–46.

Lent, R. W., Lopez, F. G., Brown, S. D., & Gore, P. A. (1996). Latent structure of the sources of mathematics self-efficacy. *Journal of Vocational Behavior, 49*(3), 292–308.

Linnenbrink, E. A., & Pintrich, P. R. (2000). Multiple pathways to learning and achievement: The role of goal orientation in fostering adaptive motivation, affect, and cognition. In C. Sansone & J. Harackiewicz (Eds.), *Intrinsic and extrinsic motivation: The search for optimal motivation and performance* (pp. 195–227). San Diego, CA: Academic Press.

Lloyd, J. E. V., Walsh, J., & Yailagh, M. S. (2005). Sex differences in performance attributions, self-efficacy, and achievement in mathematics: If I'm so smart, why don't I know it? *Canadian Journal of Education, 28*(3), 384–408.

Locke, E. A., & Latham, G. P. (2002). Building a practically useful theory of goal setting and task motivation: A 35-year odyssey. *American Psychologist, 57*(9), 705–717.

Mallow, J. (1991). Reading science. *Journal of Reading, 34*(5), 324–338.

Mallow, J. (2006). *Science anxiety: Research and action.* Arlington, VA: National Science Teacher Association. Retrieved from http://learning center.nsta.org/files/PB205X-1.pdf

Mallow, J. (2010, September). *Gender, science anxiety, and science attitudes: A multinational perspective.* Paper presented at the meeting of the United Nations Division for the Advancement of Women, United Nations Educational, Scientific and Cultural Organization (UNESCO), Paris, France.

Mangels, J. A., Good, C., Whiteman, R. C., Maniscalco, B., & Dweck, C. S. (2012). Emotion blocks the path to learning under stereotype threat. *Social Cognitive and Affective Neuroscience, 7*(2), 230–241.

Meece, J. L., Anderman, E. M., & Anderman, L. H. (2006). Classroom goal structure, student motivation, and academic achievement. *Annual Review of Psychology, 57*, 487–503.

Midgley, C., Feldlaufer, H., & Eccles, J. S. (1989). Student/teacher relations and attitudes toward mathematics before and after the transition to junior high school. *Child Development, 60*(4), 981–992.

Mikami, A. Y., Gregory, A., Allen, J. P., Pianta, R. C., & Lun, J. (2011). Effects of a teacher professional development intervention on peer relationships in secondary classrooms. *School Psychology Review, 40*(3), 367–385.

Miller, D. (1998). *Enhancing adolescent competence.* Belmont, CA: Wadsworth.

Mowrer, O. H. (1960). *Learning theory and behavior.* New York, NY: Wiley.

Murray, H. A. (1938). *Explorations in personality.* New York, NY: Oxford University Press.

National Science Board. (2004). Public knowledge about science and technology. *Science and Engineering Indicators 2004* (NSB Report No. 04–01). Arlington, VA: (NSB 04–01). Retrieved from http://www.nsf.gov/statistics/seind04/c7/c7s2.htm

National Science Teachers Association. (2004). *NSTA position statement on scientific inquiry.* Retrieved from http://www.nsta.org/about/positions/inquiry.aspx

Nguyen, H. D., & Ryan, A. M. (2008). Does stereotype threat affect test performance of minorities and women? A meta-analysis of experimental evidence. *Journal of Applied Psychology, 93*(6), 1314–1334.

Niemiec, C., & Ryan, R. (2009). Autonomy, competence, and relatedness in the classroom: Applying self-determination theory to educational practice. *Theory and Research in Education, 7*(2), 133–144.

Nolen, S., & Haladyna, T. (1990). Motivation and studying in high school science. *Journal of Research in Science Teaching, 27*(2), 115–126.

Pajares, F. (n.d.). *But they did not give up.* Retrieved from http://www.uky.edu/~eushe2/Pajares/OnFailingG.html

Pajares, F., Johnson, M. J., & Usher, E. L. (2007). Sources of writing self-efficacy beliefs of elementary, middle, and high school students. *Research in the Teaching of English, 42*(1), 104–120.

Palmer, D. (2007). What is the best way to motivate students in science? *Teaching Science, 53*(1), 38–42.

Patrick, H., Anderman, L. H., & Ryan, A. M. (2002). Social motivation and the classroom social environment. In C. Midgley (Ed.), *Goals, goal structures, and patterns of adaptive learning* (pp. 85–108). Mahwah, NJ: Lawrence Erlbaum.

Pekrun, R. (1992). The impact of emotions on learning and achievement: Towards a theory of cognitive/motivational mediators. *Applied Psychology, 41*(4), 359–376.

Pekrun, R., Elliot, A., & Maier, M. (2009). Achievement goals and achievement emotions: Testing a model of their joint relations with academic performance. *Journal of Educational Psychology, 101*(1), 115–135.

Pekrun, R., Frenzel, A. C., Goetz, T., & Perry, R. P. (2007). The control-value theory of achievement emotions: An integrative approach to emotions in education. In P. A. Schutz & R. Pekrun (Eds.), *Emotion in education.* Burlington, MA: Academic Press.

Pekrun, R., Goetz, T., Frenzel, A. C., Barchfield, P., & Perry, R. P. (2011). Measuring emotions in students' learning and performance: The achievement emotions questionnaire (AEQ). *Contemporary Educational Psychology, 36*(1), 36–48.

Pekrun, R., Goetz, T., Titz, W., & Perry, R. P. (2002). Academic emotions in students' self-regulated learning and achievement: A program of qualitative and quantitative research. *Educational Psychologist, 37*(2), 91–105.

Pianta, R. C. (1999). *Enhancing relationships between children and teachers.* Washington, DC: American Psychological Association.

Pintrich, P. R. (2000). Multiple goals, multiple pathways: The role of goal orientation in learning and achievement. *Journal of Educational Psychology, 92*(3), 544–555.

Pintrich, P. R. (2003). A motivational science perspective on the role of student motivation in learning and teaching contexts. *Journal of Educational Psychology, 95*(4), 667–686.

Posner, M., & Rothbart, M. K. (2007). *Educating the human brain.* Washington, DC: American Psychological Association.

Pugh, K., Linnenbrink-Garcia, L., Koskey, K., Stewart, V., & Manzey, C. (2010). Motivation, learning, and transformative experience: A study of deep engagement in science. *Science Education, 94*(1), 1–28.

Purdie-Vaughns, V. (2012, June). *Broadening participation and STEM: Stereotype threat.* Plenary session presented at the 2012 Joint Annual Meeting Broadening Participation Research, National Science Foundation, Washington, DC.

Ratelle, C. F., Larose, S., Guay, F., & Senecal, C. (2005). Perceptions of parental involvement and support as predictors of college students' persistence in a science curriculum. *Journal of Family Psychology, 19*(2), 286–293.

Reeve, J. (2006). Teachers as facilitators: What autonomy-supportive teachers do and why their students benefit. *Elementary School Journal, 106*(3), 225–236.

Reeve, J., Bolt, E., & Cai, Y. (1999). Autonomy-supportive teachers: How they teach and motivate students. *Journal of Educational Psychology, 91*(3), 537–548.

Reeve, J., & Halusic, M. (2009). How K–12 teachers can put self-determination theory principles into practice. *Theory and Research in Education, 7*(2), 145–154.

Reeve, J., & Jang, H. (2006). What teachers say and do to support students' autonomy during a learning activity. *Journal of Educational Psychology, 98*(1), 209–218.

Renninger, K. (1992). Individual interest and development: Implications for theory and practice. In K. A. Renninger, S. Hidi, & A. Krapp (Eds.), *The role of interest in learning and development* (pp. 361–396). New York, NY: Taylor & Francis.

Renninger, K. A., & Hidi, S. (2011). Revisiting the conceptualization, measurement, and generation of interest. *Educational Psychologist, 46*(3), 168–184.

Robinson, M., & Ochs, G. (2008). Determining why students take more science than required in high school. *Bulletin of Science, Technology & Society, 28*(4), 338–348.

Rodriguez, C. (2012, June). *Broadening participation and STEM: Challenges and opportunities.* Plenary session presented at the 2012 Joint Annual Meeting: Broadening Participation Research, National Science Foundation, Washington, DC.

Ryan, R., & Brown, K. (2005). Legislating competence: High-stakes testing policies and their relations with psychological theories and research. In A. J. Elliot & C. S. Dweck (Eds.), *Handbook of competence and motivation* (pp. 354–372). New York, NY: Guilford Publications.

Ryan, R. M., & Deci, E. L. (2000a). Intrinsic and extrinsic motivations: Classic definitions and new directions. *Contemporary Educational Psychology, 25,* 54–67.

Ryan, R. M., & Deci, E. L. (2000b). Self-determination theory and the facilitation of intrinsic motivation, social development, and well-being. *American Psychologist, 55*(1), 68–78.

Rydell, R. J., Shiffrin, R. M., Boucher, K. L., Van Loo, K., & Rydell, M. T. (2010). Stereotype threat prevents perceptual learning. *Proceedings of the National Academy of Sciences, 107*(32), 14042–14047.

Sadker, D., Sadker, M., & Zittleman, K. (2009). *Still failing at fairness: How gender bias cheats boys and girls in school and what we can do about it.* New York, NY: Scribner.

Sanders, J. (2010). Lessons I have learned in three decades of working with teachers about girls in STEM. *Journal of Women in Science and Engineering, 16*(2), 99–113.

Savery, J. R., & Duffy, T. M. (1996). Problem based learning: An instructional model and its constructivist framework. In B. Wilson (Ed.), *Constructivist learning environments: Case studies in instructional design* (pp. 135–148). Englewood Cliffs, NJ: Educational Technology.

Schiefele, U. (2009). Situational and individual interest. In K. Wentzel & A. Wigfield (Eds.), *Handbook of motivation at school* (pp. 197–222). New York, NY: Routledge.

Schmader, T., Johns, M., & Forbes, C. (2008). An integrated process model of stereotype threat effects on performance. *Psychological Review, 115*(2), 336–356.

Schmidt, J. A., Kackar, H. Z., & Strati, A. D. (2010, May). *Do motivational processes "work" differently for male and females students in science? Examining the role of situational factors and gender in motivational processes among high school science students.* Paper presented at the annual meeting of the American Educational Research Association, Denver, CO.

Schmidt, J. A., & Shumow, L. (2012). Change in self-efficacy in high school science classrooms: An analysis by gender. In S. L. Britner (Ed.), *Psychology of self-efficacy* (pp. 53–74). Hauppauge, NY: Nova Science Publishers.

Schmidt, J. A., Strati, A. D., & Kackar, H. Z. (2010, March). *Similar and different: Comparisons of males' and females' achievement, attitudes, interest, and experience in high school science.* Poster presented at the biennial meeting of the Society for Research on Adolescence, Philadelphia, PA.

Schmidt, J. A., Zaleski, D. J., Shumow, L., Ochoa-Angrino, S., & Hamidova, N. (2011, April). *What are they really doing? A descriptive analysis of science teachers' instructional practices and verbal interactions with students.* Paper presented at the annual meeting of the American Educational Research Association, New Orleans, LA.

Schunk, D. H. (1989). Self-efficacy and achievement behaviors. *Educational Psychology Review, 1,* 173–208.

Schunk, D. H. (2011). *Learning theories: An educational perspective* (6th ed.). Upper Saddle River, NJ: Prentice Hall.

Schunk, D. H., & Hanson, A. R. (1985). Peer models: Influence on children's self-efficacy and achievement. *Journal of Educational Psychology, 77,* 313–322.

Schunk, D. H, & Miller, S. (2002). Self-efficacy and adolescents' motivation. In F. Pajares & T. Urdan (Eds.), *Academic motivation of adolescents* (pp. 29–51). Greenwich, CT: Information Age Publishing.

Schunk, D. H., Pintrich, P. R., & Meece, J. L. (2008). *Motivation in education: Theory, research, and applications.* Upper Saddle River, NJ: Prentice Hall.

Seligman, M. E. (2004). Can happiness be taught? *Daedalus, 133*(2), 80–87.

Shernoff, D. J., Csikszentmihalyi, M., Schneider, B., & Shernoff, E. S. (2003). Student engagement in high school classrooms from the perspective of flow theory. *School Psychology Quarterly, 18*(2), 158–176.

Shernoff, D. J., & Schmidt, J. A. (2008). Further evidence of an engagement-achievement paradox among U.S. high school students. *Journal of Youth and Adolescence, 37*(5), 564–580.

Shumow, L., Lyutykh, E., & Schmidt, J. A. (2011). Predictors and outcomes of parent involvement with high school students in science. *The School Community Journal, 21*(2), 81–98.

Shumow, L., & Miller, J. (2001). Parents' at-home and at-school academic involvement with young adolescents. *Journal of Early Adolescence, 21*(1), 68–91.

Shumow, L., & Schmidt, J. A. (2013). Academic grades and motivation in high school science classrooms among male and female students: Associations with teachers' characteristics, beliefs, and practices. In R. Haumann & G. Zimmer (Eds.), *Handbook of academic performance predictors, learning strategies, and influence of gender.* Hauppauge, NY: Nova Science Publishers.

Shumow, L., Schmidt, J. A., & Darfler, A. (2010, May). *"Talking the talk" and "walking the walk": Exploring high school science teachers' belief systems and classroom practices regarding gender and science.* Paper presented at the annual meeting of the American Educational Research Association, Denver, CO.

Shumow, L., Schmidt, J. A., & Zaleski, D. (2013). Multiple perspectives on student learning, engagement, and motivation in high school biology labs. *The High School Journal, 96*(3), 232–252.

Simon, B. (2001). Family involvement in high school: Predictors and effects. *NASSP Bulletin, 85*(627), 8–19.

Slavin, R. (2000). *Computing improvement points.* Retrieved from http://www.abacon.com/slavin/t89.html

Society of Women Engineers-Assessing Women and Men in Engineering Project (SWE-AWE). (2009). *Gender differences in science achievement* [Information Sheet]. Retrieved June 23, 2011 from www.AWEonline.org.

Sorby, S. A. (2009). Educational research in developing 3-D spatial skills for engineering students. *International Journal of Science Education, 31*(3), 459–480.

Sorby, S. A., & Baartmans, B. J. (2000). The development and assessment of a course for enhancing the 3-D spatial visualization skills of first year engineering students. *Journal of Engineering Education, 89*(3), 301–307.

Spencer, S., Steele, C. M., & Quinn, D. M. (1999). Stereotype threat and women's math performance. *Journal of Experimental Social Psychology, 35*(1), 4–28.

Stambor, Z. (2006). How laughing leads to learning. *Monitor on Psychology, 37*(6), 62–66.

Steele, C. M. (1997). A threat in the air: How stereotypes shape intellectual identity and performance. *American Psychologist, 52*(6), 613–629.

Steele, C. M., & Aronson, J. (1995). Stereotype threat and the intellectual test performance of African-Americans. *Journal of Personality and Social Psychology, 69*(5), 797–811.

Steinberg, L. (2008). *Adolescence.* Boston, MA: McGraw-Hill.

Steinberg, L., Lamborn, S. D., Dornbusch, S. M., & Darling, N. (1992). Impact of parenting practices on adolescent achievement: Authoritative parenting, school involvement, and encouragement to succeed. *Child Development, 63*(5), 1266–1281.

Stipek, D. (1998). *Motivation to learn: From theory to practice* (3rd ed.). Boston, MA: Allyn & Bacon.

Strati, A. D. (2011, April). *Exploring the role of teacher support and situational variables on high school students' academic engagement, success, and anxiety in science.* Paper presented at the annual meeting of the American Educational Research Association, New Orleans, LA.

Strati, A. D., & Schmidt, J. A. (2012, April). *Exploring the role of teacher challenge and support on high school students' academic engagement in physics classrooms.* Paper presented at the annual meeting of the American Educational Research Association, Vancouver, B.C.

Strati, A. D., & Schmidt, J. A. (2013, April). *Exploring the role of teacher challenge and support in high school general science classrooms.* Paper presented at the annual meetings of the American Educational Research Association, San Francisco, CA.

Stuhlman, M., Hamre, B., Downer, J., & Pianta, R. (2012). *What should classroom observations measure? A practitioner's guide to conducting classroom observations.* Retrieved from University of Virginia, The Center for the Advanced Study of Teaching and Learning. Retrieved from http://curry.virginia.edu/uploads/resourceLibrary/CASTL_practioner_Part2_single.pdf

Sun, R. C. F., & Hui, E. K. P. (2007). Psychosocial factors contributing to adolescent suicidal ideation. *Journal of Youth Adolescence, 36*(6), 775–786.

Suresh, S. (2012, June). *Welcome to plenary session,* presented at the 2012 Joint Annual Meeting, Broadening Participation Research, National Science Foundation, Washington, DC.

Tomlinson, C. A., & Strickland, C. A. (2005). *Differentiation in practice: A resource guide for differentiating curriculum, grades 9–12.* Alexandria, VA: Association for Supervision & Curriculum Development.

Turner, J. C., Meyer, D. K., Midgley, C., & Patrick, H. (2003). Teacher discourse and sixth graders' reported affect and achievement behaviors in two high-mastery/high-performance mathematics classrooms. *The Elementary School Journal, 103*(4), 357–382.

Urdan, T., & Midgley, C. (2003). Changes in the perceived classroom goal structure and pattern of adaptive learning during early adolescence. *Contemporary Educational Psychology, 28*(4), 524–551.

VandeWalle, D. (1997). Development and validation of a work domain goal orientation instrument, *Educational and Psychological Measurement, 57*(6), 995–1015.

Velayutham, S., Aldridge, J., & Fraser, B. (2012). Gender differences in student motivation and self-regulation in science learning: A multigroup structural equation modeling analysis. *International Journal of Science and Mathematics Education, 10*(6), 1347–1368.

Vygotsky, L. S. (1962). *Thought and language.* Cambridge, MA: MIT Press.

Weiner, B. (1986). *An attributional theory of motivation and emotion.* New York, NY: Springer-Verlag.

Weiner, B. (1992). *Human motivation: Metaphors, theories and research.* Newbury Park, CA: SAGE.

Weinstein, C. (2003). *Secondary classroom management: Lessons from research and practice.* Boston, MA: McGraw-Hill.

Wentzel, K. R. (1997). Student motivation in middle school: The role of perceived pedagogical caring. *Journal of Educational Psychology, 89*(3), 411–419.

Wentzel, K. R. (2002). Are effective teachers like good parents? Teaching styles and student adjustment in early adolescence. *Child Development, 73*(1), 287–301.

Wentzel, K. R., & Battle, A. A. (2001). Social relationships and school adjustment. In T. Urdan & F. Pajares (Eds.), *Adolescence and education: General issues in the education of adolescents* (pp. 93–118). Greenwich, CT: Information Age Publishing.

Wentzel, K. R., Battle, A., Russell, S. L., & Looney, L. B. (2010). Social supports from teachers and peers as predictors of academic and social motivation. *Contemporary Educational Psychology, 35*(3), 193–202.

White, R. W. (1959). Motivation reconsidered: The concept of competence. *Psychological Review, 66*(5), 297–333.

Wigfield, A., & Eccles, J. S. (2000). Expectancy-value theory of achievement motivation. *Contemporary Educational Psychology, 25*(1), 68–81.

Wigfield, A., & Eccles, J. S. (2002). The development of competence beliefs and values from childhood through adolescence. In A. Wigfield & J. S. Eccles (Eds.), *Development of achievement motivation* (pp. 92–120). San Diego, CA: Academic Press.

Wigfield, A., & Tonks, S. (2002). Adolescents' expectancies for success and achievement task values during the middle and high school years. In F. Pajares & T. Urdan (Eds.), *Academic motivation of adolescents* (pp. 53–82). Greenwich CT: Information Age Publishing.

Williams, D. A., & King, P. (1980, December 15). Do males have a math gene? *Newsweek, 96,* 73.

Williams, G. C., & Deci, E. L. (1996). Internalization of biopsychosocial values by medical students: A test of self-determination theory. *Journal of Personality and Social Psychology, 70*(4), 767–779.

Willms, J. D., Friesen, S., & Milton, P. (2009). *What did you do in school today? Transforming classrooms through social, academic, and intellectual engagement* (First National Report). Toronto, ON: Canadian Education Association.

Wingate, U. (2006). Doing away with "study skills." *Teaching in Higher Education, 11*(4), 457–469.

Wong, M. M. (2008). Perceptions of parental involvement and autonomy support: Their relations with self-regulation, academic performance, substance use and resilience among adolescents. *North American Journal of Psychology, 10*(3), 497–518.

Zaleski, D. J. (2012). *The influence of momentary classroom goal structures on student engagement and achievement in high school science* (Unpublished doctoral dissertation). Northern Illinois University, DeKalb, IL.

Zaleski, D. J, & Lyutykh, E. (2012, November). *Five shows a day five days a week: Humor and engagement in high school science.* Paper presented at the Mid-Western Educational Research Association Annual Meeting, Evanston, IL.

Zeldin, A. L., & Pajares, F. (2000). Against the odds: Self-efficacy beliefs of women in mathematical, scientific, and technological careers. *American Educational Research Journal, 37*(1), 215–246.

Zhang, M., Kochler, M., Lundeberg, M., Eberhardt, J., & Parker, J. (2010, May). *Understanding science teachers' needs for professional development.* Poster presented at the annual meeting of the American Educational Research Association, Denver, CO.

Zusho, A., Pintrich, P. W., & Coppola, B. (2003). Skill and will: The role of motivation and cognition in the learning of college chemistry. *International Journal of Science Education, 25*(9), 1081–1094.

Zuzanek, J. (1999). *Experience sampling method: Current and potential research applications.* Paper presented at the workshop on time-use measurement and research, National Research Council, Washington, DC.

Index

Figures are indicated by f following the page number.

Ability beliefs
  defined, 95–97
  fostering of, 104–109, 107f
  gender differences in, 8–10, 9f
  importance of, 97–100, 98f
  mindset and, 96
  research on, 100–104, 102f
  resources for promoting, 109
  stereotype threats and,
    96–97, 99–100
  student-teacher relationships
    and, 33–34
  value and, 19
Ability-focused orientation, 80
Ability grouping, 91–92
Activating emotions, 126
Active learning, 87
Activities
  challenge and, 116–118, 117f
  emotions and, 129–130, 130f
  types of, 3–4f, 3–5
  See also Lab activities
Activity-focused positive
    emotions, 126
Affiliation. *See* Relationships
Age, interest declining with, 16
Anxiety. *See* Emotions
Assessment, 87, 89–91, 90f, 121
Attainment value, 15
Attribution, 68–71, 73–74, 74f
Autonomy
  defined, 41
  fostering of, 43, 49–53, 49f

importance of, 42–43
research on, 44–49, 44f
resources for promoting, 54

Bias, 10, 103–104, 108–109.
  See also Gender differences;
  Stereotype threats
Brain function, 102–103, 105
Brainology Program, 105
Bullying, 39
Bureaucracy, 31–32

Caring, instrumental support as, 29
Challenge
  defined, 111–112
  engagement and, 115–116,
    116f, 119f
  fostering of, 119–122
  importance of, 112–113, 113f
  research on, 114–119,
    116–117f, 119f
  resources for promoting, 123
Choice, 45, 50–51
Classroom activities breakdown,
    3–4f, 3–5
Classroom climate
  overview of, 29
  confidence and, 57
  fostering positive, 38–39
  learning dependent on,
    31, 34–35, 34f
Classroom structure, 52, 83
Cognitive coping skills, 108

Collaboration, 30
Communication, 51–52, 64,
    72, 120–122
Competence, 33–34, 68, 76.
    See also Ability beliefs
Confidence
    defined, 56
    fostering of, 62–64
    importance of, 56–57, 57f
    research on, 57–62
    resources for promoting, 65
    success and, 69
Constructive feedback. See Feedback
Control, 44–45, 50–53
Cooperative learning, 35
Coping skills, 108, 134–136
Cost value, 15–16
Cultural relevance, 24–25

Danger anxiety, 126
Deactivating emotions, 126
Differentiated instruction,
    91–92, 121–122

Effort.
    as internal, 70–71
    learning attributions and,
        69–70, 74f
    mindset and, 98–99,
        98f, 102, 118
    role models for, 63–64
    See also Challenge
Ego-focused orientation, 80
Emotional support, 28
Emotions
    confidence and, 59
    defined, 125
    fostering of enjoyment, 134–136
    gender differences in,
        60, 132–133, 132f
    importance of studying,
        127–129, 127f
    range of, 125–127
    research on, 129–134, 130–132f
    resources for improving, 137
    subject area and, 131–132
Encouragement. See Persuasion

Engagement
    Experience Sampling Method used
        to measure, 5–6
    gender differences in,
        8–10, 9f
    interest and, 16
    teacher support and, 33–34
Enthusiasm, 24
Equity, 11, 37, 61
Errors, 88, 105–106
Expectations, 120
Experience Sampling Method (ESM),
    5–6, 143–144
External attribution, 68
Extrinsic motivation, 1, 46–48

Failure, 85, 105–106
Family involvement
    autonomy and, 48–49
    autonomy promotion and, 53
    challenge and, 122
    communication about, 64, 72
    confidence promotion and, 62
    goal orientation and, 86, 92
    success and, 72, 76
    valuing of science by students and,
        18–19, 25
Fear. See Emotions
Feedback
    autonomy and, 50
    goal orientation and, 89, 90f
    inquiry approach and, 48
    persuasion as, 59
    success and, 69–70
    wise feedback, 106–107
Feelings about science, 9f
Fishbowl, 39
Fixed mindsets, 96, 98f, 118.
    See also Stereotype threats

Gender differences
    awareness of, xvii–xviii
    challenge and, 118–119, 119f
    choices in activities and, 45
    competence recognition and, 76
    confidence and, 56–57, 59
    emotions and, 60, 132–133, 132f

experience of science, 8–10, 9f
goal orientation and, 85
interest and, 20
mastery experiences and, 59–60
mindset and, 98–99,
    101–102, 102f
motivation and, 6–8, 7f
science anxiety and, 133–134
success perception and, 71–72
teacher behaviors and, 32–33
teacher bias and, 10, 103
value and, 20
Gender equity, 11, 37, 61
Gifted students, fixed mindsets
    and, 106
Goal orientation
defined, 79–80
fostering of, 86–92, 90f
importance of, 80–83, 81f
research on, 83–86, 85f
resources for promoting, 93
types of, 80
Goal setting, 67–68, 75
Group work, 39, 91–92
Growth mindsets
challenge and, 118, 121
defined, 96
fixed mindsets compared, 98f
mastery goal orientation and, 88
resources for promoting, 109

Helpless orientation, 81–82
Higher-order thinking, 87

Identity development, 17, 36
Independence. *See* Autonomy
Individual interest, 14, 20–21
Inquiry approach, 43, 48,
    52–53, 86–87
Instrumental support, 28–29, 38
Interest
defined, 13
gender differences in, 20
individual interest, 14, 20–21
situational interest, 14, 17–18,
    21–22
Internal attribution, 68

Intrinsic motivation, 1–2, 46–47.
    See also Challenge
Intrinsic value, 13–14

Lab activities
challenge and, 116–118, 117f
emotions and, 129–130, 130f
relevance of, 21–23, 22f
Language, invitational versus
    controlling, 51
Learning
about students, 36–37
active, 87
classroom climate and,
    31, 34–35, 34f
cooperative, 35
emotions and, 127–128
problem-based learning, 23–24
Learning-focused orientation, 80

Mastery experiences, 57–60
Mastery goal orientation, 80–81
Mathematics anxiety, 127
Mindfulness interventions, 108, 136
Mindset
overview of, 96, 98f
challenge and, 118, 121
effort beliefs and, 98–99,
    98f, 102, 118
persistence and, 100
See also Ability beliefs; Goal
    orientation
Mistakes, 88, 105–106
Modeling
about challenges, 120–121
confidence and, 58, 63–64
gender and, 32
stereotype threats and, 107–108
Motivation
extrinsic motivation, 1, 46–48
gender differences in, 6–8, 7f
intrinsic motivation, 1–2, 46–47
as state, 1
See also Challenge

Next Generation Science Standards
    (NGSS), xix

Observations, 58, 144–145
Outcome-focused positive
    emotions, 126

Parent involvement.
    See Family involvement
Participation, increasing, 38
PBL (problem-based learning),
    23–24
Peer relationships, 29f, 35–36
Performance anxiety, 127
Performance approach goal
    orientation, 80
Performance avoidance goal
    orientation, 80
Performance goal orientation,
    80, 81–82
Persistence, mindset and, 100
Persuasion, 47–48, 58–60, 64
Physiological responses, 59
Planning, for group work, 39
Positive self-talk, 135
Praise or recognition
    autonomy and, 47
    of effort, 104
    mastery goal orientation and,
        89–91, 90f
    success and, 70
    See also Extrinsic motivation
Pride, success and, 69
Prior successes, 57–60
Problem-based learning (PBL),
    23–24
Process feedback, 70
Procrastination, 82
Professional development, 43
Punishments, 47

Reappraisal, 108
Recognition or praise. *See* Praise or
    recognition
Reflection, on value, 23
Relationships
    fostering of, 36–39
    goal orientation and, 92
    importance of, 30–31
    ingredients for, 28–29

between peers, 29, 29f, 35–36
    research on, 31–36, 34f
    resources for promoting,
        39–40
Relaxation responses, 136
Relevance, 16, 21–23, 22f
Research
    ability beliefs, 100–104, 102f
    autonomy, 44–49, 44f
    challenge, 114–119,
        116–117f, 119f
    confidence, 57–62
    emotions, 129–134, 130–132f
    goal orientation, 83–86, 85f
    relationships, 31–36, 34f
    success, 70–72
    value, 17–20
Rewards, 46–47. *See also* Extrinsic
    motivation
Role models. *See* Modeling

Science anxiety, 126–127.
    See also Emotions
Science-in-the-Moment Project
    (SciMO)
    overview of, 2
    activities and emotions,
        129–130, 130f
    autonomy support and, 45–46
    classroom activities breakdown,
        3–4f, 3–5
    context for, 139
    control and, 44
    data coding, 146
    data collection, 142–145
    Experience Sampling Method used
        for, 5–6
    goal orientation and,
        84–85, 85f
    participants in, 139–141,
        140–142f
    success and, 72
    teacher talk, 4–5, 4f
Scientific literacy, 11, 136
Scientists, advice from, 23
SciMO. *See* Science-in-the-Moment
    Project (SciMO)

Seatwork, 3, 3f, 45, 130f
Self-determination theory (SDT), 42, 68
Self-efficacy. *See* Confidence
Self-talk, 135
Situational interest, 14, 17–18, 21–22
Skill, challenge and, 116, 116f
Spatial skills, 75–76
Squeamish anxiety, 126
Stereotype threats
  overview of, 96–97
  alleviating, 103–104, 106–109, 107f
  damage from, 99–100
  mindset and, 101–103
  resources for reducing, 109
Storytelling, 24
Stress. *See* Emotions
Struggles, 105–106
Student identity development, 17
Student perspectives
  Experience Sampling Method used to measure, 5–6
  gender differences in, 6–8, 7f
  recognition of, 50
  soliciting of, 38
  teacher attention to, 28
  value in science lacking, 17–18
Students, 36–37, 105–106
Student-teacher relationships. *See* Relationships
Study buddies, 75
Study skills, 81–82, 87–88, 135–136
Subgoals, 75
Success
  defined, 67–68
  fostering of, 72–76, 73–74f
  importance of, 69–70
  promoting, 62
  research on, 70–72
  resources for promoting, 77
Support
  autonomy, 45–46, 49–53, 49f
  emotional, 28
  engagement and, 33–34
  fostering of, 36–39
  instrumental, 28–29, 38
  perceptions of, 33

Task-focused orientation, 80
Teacher resources
  ability beliefs and, 109
  autonomy and, 54
  for background information, 11–12
  challenge and, 123
  confidence and, 65
  emotions and, 137
  goal orientation and, 93
  growth mindsets and, 109
  relationships and, 39–40
  stereotype threats and, 109
  success and, 77
  value and, 25–26
Teachers
  autonomy promotion, 43, 49–53, 49f
  confidence promotion and, 61–62
  relationship promotion, 36–39
  student gender and interactions, 10
  thought experiment for, 6–8, 7f
  value promotion, 18
  See also Relationships
Teacher sensitivity, 28
Teasing, 39
Test anxiety, 127, 130–131
Test taking, 18, 116–117, 117f, 136
Thought experiment, 6–8, 7f
Time, use of, 88–89
Tutors, 75

Utility value, 14–15

Value
  attainment value, 15
  cost value, 15–16
  fostering of, 20–25, 22f
  gender differences in, 20
  importance of, 16–17

    intrinsic value, 13–14
    research on, 17–20
    resources for promoting, 25–26
    utility value, 14–15
Vicarious experiences, 58
Visualization, 75–76

Website, xx
Wise feedback,
    106–107

Zone of proximal
    development, 113

CORWIN

A SAGE Company

The Corwin logo—a raven striding across an open book—represents the union of courage and learning. Corwin is committed to improving education for all learners by publishing books and other professional development resources for those serving the field of PreK–12 education. By providing practical, hands-on materials, Corwin continues to carry out the promise of its motto: **"Helping Educators Do Their Work Better."**